Spiritual *Principles* FOR A

PROSPEROUS LIFE

ROBERT HENDERSON JR. CFP®

Cover Design & Illustrations by Ralph Williams
Chris1 Graphic Design, Inc.
Edited by Arlene W. Robinson

Library of Congress Control Number:
ISBN 978-1-4536-1189-0
Printed in the United States of America

Acknowledgements:

Special thanks

Rev. Dr. Mary Tumpkin
Thank you for welcoming and supporting this idea from the
start. I have learned a great deal from you over the many years

My personal assistant and daughter, Hyacinth whom I am very
proud of and blessed to have the opportunity to
work with over the years

All the ministers and teachers that have dedicated time and
work into making this project come to fruition; your
patience was greatly appreciated

Dedications

To my loving mother, Johnnie Mae Henderson
who taught me perseverance, love and fairness

To my loving wife, Natalie, for her patience,
love and endless support

Forward

Robert Henderson Jr. CFP

Today we are living in a time where people from all over the world are looking and searching for answers and ways to help live a more harmonious, spiritual and prosperous life. Although we are living in the age of information and technology, many people are learning and studying, but still unable to come to the realization of truth. By truth, I mean, the understanding of one's self. The major problem that most of all of mankind faces today is, the lack of, and the misunderstanding of the inherited inner power that each of us possess. Many people don't know where to turn to or look for the proper guidance and support. Many people spend years searching for answers in things and stuff, only to find that material things can only satisfy that which is material, and all that which is spirit, can only be satisfied by that which is spiritual. We must begin to study the most powerful creation of all time-self. Now is the time for mankind to begin to unlock the hidden treasures of self and demonstrate the unlimited powers of our inner self.

This book is designed for anyone who is seeking guidance and support in obtaining harmony, peace, love, health and a prosperous life. It is for those who have a thirst for seeking and finding The Kingdom of The Almighty within themselves. In order to find, you must be willing to seek. This book is for those who are seeking, knocking and asking for more. It is not, I repeat, this book is not for the traditional thinker, rather it's written for those who are willing to leave their comfort zone and explore new thoughts and new ideas. The chapters are filled with information to encourage and up lift you to a higher consciousness. Ten authors and ministers from around the country who practice New Thought and Metaphysical Principles have come together to share these Spiritual Principles to help guide and lead you in achieving a prosperous life. In this book you will find at the beginning of each lesson, (and yes, these are lessons), the writer's bio as well as their contact information to be used for further insight on their lesson. These lessons are not designed or written to be a quick read; they are written to be studied. We highly recommend that you read and re-read these lessons until they become a part of your consciousness. When it becomes a part of your consciousness, you will be able to demonstrate the principles. Many people read and study and yet, can't demonstrate that which they profess to know. Trust me, for it is written, it is impossible to truly know something and not be able to demonstrate it. The chapters and lessons in this book have been carefully selected to address key spiritual principles that must be incorporated and made a part of your daily living. You can be financially well off and still not be prosperous or at peace because something or someone has offended you in the past and you haven't forgiven them. Holding on to the past can really put a damper on the future. This is why the lesson on The Power of Forgiveness is essential to a truly wonderful prosperous life. When we use the term prosperous, we don't particularly mean money, for us, the word prosperous means to flow, in harmony. Just as water flows down the river and the seasons change, we believe we all must begin to flow, grow and change.

Robert Henderson Jr.
Certified Financial Planner®

Table of Contents

Table of Contents

-Continued-

About The Author

The Rev. Dr. Mary Tumpkin, President of the Universal Foundation for Better Living and Senior Minister of the Universal Truth Center for Better Living in Miami Gardens, Florida, is a widely acclaimed teacher/minister/Bible scholar who has lectured throughout the United States as well as England, Canada, South America, Spain, and the Caribbean. Some of Dr. Tumpkin's teachings are chronicled in her publications Tithing: Are You Ready?, Before You Pray—Forgive, and Do You Know the Secret?: Understanding the Spiritual Nature of the Law of Attraction. Dr. Tumpkin currently serves on the Boards of the International New Thought Alliance (INTA), the Jesus Seminar, The Society for the Study of Metaphysical Religion and the Miami Coalition of Christians and Jews.

Rev. Dr. Mary A. Tumpkin
Universal Truth Center for Better Living
21310 N.W. 37th Avenue
Miami Gardens, Florida 33056
305.624.4991
www.utruthcenter.org
mtumpkin@aol.com

- One -

The Power of Tithing

By The Rev. Dr. Mary Tumpkin

Most of us have been taught to define success in terms of what we can acquire and achieve. Spiritual wisdom dictates that the opposite is true; our well-being is established based on what we are able to give. Making such a transition in thought requires new insights into who we are and what our purpose is. Tithing is a highly useful discipline that helps us discover the joy of giving. The subject of tithing usually elicits one of two responses: distaste or magical expectation. Hopefully, after reading this chapter, both the magic of and the distaste for tithing will be stripped away and a new awareness acquired. Perhaps instead of thinking of tithing as either a ploy by religious organizations to increase their coffers, or a secret technique that can make us rich quickly, a new and higher concept of yourself will be developed.

`Tithing is an ancient and time-honored means by which you can expand your understanding of yourself as a participant in an opulent and abundant universe. This chapter is written to encourage you to rise from the spectator's bench and become actively involved in your own transformation.

To tithe is to give a tenth. Because most ancient cultures were agricultural, this tenth consisted of the crops reaped from harvest. The tithe was a widespread practice of many nations. In ancient Israel it was used to support the Levites and the operation of the temple (Numbers 18:21).

During his ministry, Jesus rebuked those who tithed as a compliance with the letter of the law. He encouraged his followers to go beyond outer observances and instead, seek to live fully the intention of the law (Matthew 23:23).

When we begin to study Truth and learn that no one can take anything from us, there is a hesitancy to fully believe. We need techniques that will help us break the crystallized thought patterns of those limiting beliefs. Consistent tithing causes us to look to

an inner Source, rather than outside channels, for our good. It helps us develop an attitude of gratitude as we acknowledge our inexhaustible supply. Instead of being fearful of lack, we come into a new awareness of the all-sufficiency of God.

Although the first instance of tithing mentioned in the Bible concerns the Hebrew patriarch Abraham's encounter with Melchizedek, this incident centers around the tithing of war booty. It was a onetime affair based on the success of a particular venture. However, to truly understand tithing, we must go beyond onetime deals. Abraham's grandson, Jacob, gives a more complete picture of the development of consciousness and the role of tithing.

As you remember, Jacob had conned his brother Esau into selling him his birthright. Jacob knew Esau had a definite weakness in the area of appetite. So he caught him at a vulnerable time and tempted him with a bowl of pottage (porridge). Esau, accustomed to instant gratification, bit the hook and sold out, to use the proverbial terms. But Jacob wasn't finished with his plans, because not only did he want the birthright, but also the accompanying blessing from their father Isaac. Jacob tricked his father into believing that he was his brother, Esau, by disguising himself. Even with both the birthright and the blessing, Jacob still wasn't safe, because now his brother was angry and Jacob had to flee for his life.

With the help of his mother, Rebekkah, Jacob fled his home and headed for the house of his uncle, Laban. One night during his journey, he fell asleep and had a strange dream. He saw a

4

ladder reaching from earth to heaven, and on the ladder were angels ascending and descending. He also heard a voice that blessed him and promised him success. When he rose, he proclaimed that even in that desolate place, God was present. Then he made a covenant and set a stone to commemorate his agreement. He pledged that if God would protect and provide for him, and allow him to one day return to his home in peace, then the Lord would be his God. He would then give a tenth of all that he had.

Jacob's name literally means "supplanter." He and his twin brother Esau represent the intellectual and physical aspects of our being. We are conscious of ourselves as physical beings first; hence, Esau was the first-born. Jacob represents our intellect and its struggles to assert its supremacy. This is the meaning of Jacob grabbing Esau's heel during the birthing process.

The physical aspect of ourselves is not always smart; its insistence on gratification often leads us to make unwise choices. The intellect knows the physical has this weakness, and waits for the opportunity to take away the inherent rights of the physical. Thus, at just the right time, Jacob is ready with a bowl of pottage for Esau's hunger. Because the satisfaction of the hunger is important to Esau, he sells whatever is necessary to attain it. The intellect is shrewd and cunning, and constantly plans how it will attain a superior position. It uses whatever means at its disposal to achieve its goal. It reasons that the end justifies the means, thus treachery and deception are thought to be acceptable. The blessing obtained from Isaac seals Jacob's actions with divine approval.

When we use deceptive means to acquire something, we don't always fully enjoy our acquisition: After deceiving his brother and father, Jacob couldn't stay; he had to flee the security of his home. Alone in a desolate place, he fell asleep and dreamed of a ladder reaching from earth to heaven. On the ladder there were angels ascending and descending. When he awoke, he said, "Surely the LORD is in this place and I did not know it." Jacob learned an important Truth principle—the omnipresence of God. The angels represent God; additionally, the angels moving between heaven and earth represent the availability of Divine ideas. This realization opened for Jacob the possibility of living a principle-based life. Everything manifested on "earth" begins as an idea in "heaven."

It was following this experience that Jacob decided to be a Tither. In other words, he began to learn that grasping and tricking was not the way to get ahead. The vision gave him what he needed to begin changing his thinking about his supply. His expectations were now directed toward God, since he realized that his well-being was secured by his giving, not from taking. Hollywood periodically produces a movie depicting the dead rising from their graves and moving among the living. Although these creatures exhibit mobility, they seem dazed and uncoordinated. Sadly, the "walking dead" are unconscious of their purposes and their destinies. This predicament leads to uncoordinated living.

The real-life "walking dead" have been programmed to believe the universe owes them something. So from infancy, they walk around with their hand open demanding that it be filled, and if it isn't, then they have various kinds of "tantrums." No one has bothered to explain to them that the universe doesn't allow anyone or anything to function effectively without giving.

These "walking dead" have the tendency to be in a perpetual state of rigor mortis. They hold on tightly with clenched fists, unwilling to part with any of their goods. It's no wonder they inevitably experience tight situations that forcibly pry open their hands and extract the contents. These extractions are sometimes called accidents, bad luck or misfortune. They believe some cruel force lurks in the shadows, waiting to deprive them of "their stuff."

When we awaken and become conscious of who we are, we also become aware of a different way of living. No longer do we believe that things just happen. Instead, we begin to realize there is a sense of order that governs the universe called The Law. The Law is simply the way that things work. It is impartial and impersonal. All things, including people, are required to be in harmony with it. Unlike the legal statutes that bear the same name, no one or nothing breaks or amends The Law. To become aware of its existence is a giant step in the awakening process.

The great master teacher, Jesus, simply stated a portion of The

Law in his famous Sermon on the Mount. He said, "… give, and it will be given to you. A good measure pressed down, shaken together, running over, will be put into your lap; for the measure you give will be the measure you get back" (Luke 6:38). This kind of teaching tests our sensibilities. From the human perspective, the more we give the less we have. So a restraint in our giving should mean that we will have more. The Laws of God though, are not always in line with our way of thinking. In fact, sometimes they seem downright ridiculous. But rather than reject them, we should notice how wide the gap has spread between our present understanding and the Truth.

Since The Law cannot be broken, we find ourselves suffering the consequence of our disobedience. What we do not give in a conscious, positive way is taken in ways that are not so pleasant. There is no mistake; we will give. The question is, how and to whom will we give? The "walking dead" stumble around in a daze, never knowing when something will pry open their hands. The awakened are alert and sure-footed, knowing they have the power to make the choice that will be for their highest good. Tithing is the choice of the awakened. Not because they are trying to avoid some catastrophic event, but because they know how things work. They know that no one "leeches off" the universe. So they not only open their hands to receive, but their hands remain open to give. They see themselves not as graspers, but as channels through which abundance is expressed. They know they are hooked up to a Source that gives continuously. They know that any effort to hoard simply constricts the flow.

Sometimes people approach tithing as a means to get what they want. They make elaborate wish lists, and then tithe in an attempt to force the universe to comply with their wishes. Their actions resemble the bartering one finds between customer and vendor at the flea market. To them, the universe is the vendor who sets its price, but can be bargained with by the smart buyer. Much to their chagrin, they discover that God doesn't make bargains. Notice Jacob's covenant again. He poses his agreement with God in a manner that reveals his uncertainty. "If God …," are the opening words to his testament. Many of us make such deals, or try to make such deals with God. This shows our lack of understanding of Spirit. Spirit does not cut off its supply to us for any reason. We may block our intended good by entertaining erroneous thoughts and feelings, but God has never cut any of us off. God doesn't change Its mind when we start thinking or acting better. God is, and whenever we decide to get in the flow, we receive.

What motivates us to tithe? Is it simply another scheme we are hatching to enrich ourselves? Or are we truly grateful? Our tithe should be an outer acknowledgement of gratitude for all that God is to us. If our motive is selfish, then the return we expect will never arrive. Tithing is not an attempt to convince God we are good little boys or girls. God already knows that we are Its children, and nothing we do, or do not do, will change that relationship.

There should be joy in our giving or we might as well not give. Remember Jacob? The means must be just as honorable as the end. It is wonderful and heartwarming to know we are fulfilling our roles as conscious contributors to the universe. Our lives then become proactive rather than reactive.

There is a great misunderstanding about our benevolence. For many, the tithe is categorized as a charitable gift. A charitable gift is given to meet some seeming need. It focuses on the insufficiencies of others, and it seeks to solve their problems on the level of the problem. At best, it offers first aid to a critical injury; at worst, it further cripples its recipients.

Tithing is not charity. It is not given to get the church out of the hole. Instead, it is a way of saying "Thank you" to the channel from which we have gained our spiritual inspiration. It should not be given to meet a need, but to encourage the prosperity of the ministry that helped us grow.

We give so there might be room for others who come to learn and be nourished. We give so the teacher or spiritual leader might have time to prepare and present the principles that will aid our continued growth. We give so other means may be developed to share with other seekers of the light what we have found. We give for expansion, not to prevent reduction, and in so giving, we find we are blessed.

Our tithe is not limited to monetary donations. We should also give our time and talent. Our time and talent are usually exchanged to make a living. Seldom do we take the opportunity to enhance our lives by giving freely of ourselves without thought of compensation.

Most of the jobs we perform are considered so routine, we often remark that we could do them with our eyes closed. When we give voluntarily of our time and talents, there springs up a new sense of excitement and energy. Untapped abilities rise and come forth when we knock at the door of our inner resources. We begin to learn more about ourselves and the greatness that lies within us. Often we think there is a day called "someday" somewhere on the calendar. We would love to schedule many things on that date, and we would pencil them in, if we could find it. The only "right time" is now!

Waiting for conditions "to be right" will keep you waiting a long time. There will always be a seemingly pressing need. The reason for this is that our consciousness has been based on need; we therefore draw to ourselves needy situations. One of the functions of tithing is to help us "break out" of this limiting mindset. If you now see the worth of becoming a responsible citizen of the universe, then the time is right. If you can face your fear of lack and realize that lack is only an erroneous belief you have accepted and now wish to reject, then the time is right. If you are tired of marching mindlessly with the "walking dead," then step out of formation and follow the beat of the new rhythm you hear. It is so simple and so easy if you don't resist.

There is a biblical concept called "the first fruits." It refers to giving the best to God. Since the time of Cain and Abel, the idea of the first fruits has baffled many. This concept is worthy of our consideration as we decide if we will give based on our gross or net income.

What is net income? Isn't it the amount left over after taxes, union dues, insurance payments and other deductions? In other words, the amount withheld is an investment in our government, our labor representations, and other various concerns. We should ask ourselves, how many investments do we deduct before we think about God? Should we also make our electric, gas, water and credit card payments before we decide to give our tithe? Just how far down on our list of priorities is our tithe?

As we discussed previously, the word "tithe" means "tenth." Some people find it hard at first to give at that level. Since they can't tithe, they just don't give at all.

However, there is a way to become comfortable with giving. We can consider a lesser percentage that we consistently commit to give. It might be three percent or seven percent, and so on. The important thing is to start at a point where we can give cheerfully and without anxiety. Once we have made a commitment to give this amount, we must follow through faithfully and consistently. At the same time, we can stretch our consciousness by studying the principles of prosperity and being receptive to the guidance that comes from within.

We might find, like many others, that not only do we soon become Tithers, but that we exceed the ten percent level. Believe it or not, there are those who give more than a tenth. Those people have learned the lesson that tithing teaches: There is no way you or I can ever exceed God's giving.

Notes

_____

_____

_____

_____

_____

_____

_____

_____

_____

_____

_____

- Two -

The Power of Forgiveness

By The Rev. Dr. Mary Tumpkin

For us to live effectively, we must be both inlets and outlets. For instance, breathing is not just inhalation but also exhalation. They are two sides of the same process. The water that comes in as the tide on the beach will also recede to the ocean from which it came. A recurring law that governs our prosperity teaches us that when we give, we will also receive.

Maybe we should look at forgiveness as one of those processes we must activate in our lives. Sometimes people understand forgiveness to be one-sided. They think it can only be done by a person who has reached a level of holiness that surpasses most of us average Joes and Janes. The old adage says, "To err is human; to forgive is divine." So we are quite content with categorizing forgiveness as only for those special people, few of whom walk among us. These notions might make it unlikely for the rest of us to consider Forgiveness as a natural process much like our breathing.

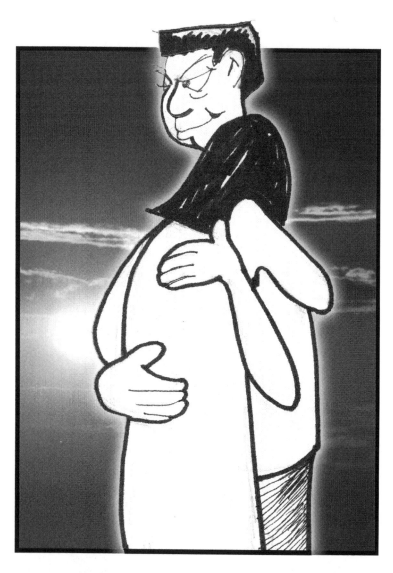

We humans have preferred to opt to another way of dealing with issues in our lives. It's called "bringing closure" to those things and persons that have offended or hurt us in any manner. Closure for us usually includes condemnation of the guilty party, and suitable punishment for their act. Often we condemn ourselves and sentence ourselves to even harsher punishment.

To progress spiritually, one must be willing to give up the false for the true. Perhaps one of the reasons why it seems so difficult for us to forgive ourselves and others is that we think we do not have the ability to do so. We perceive of ourselves as humans who are unable to function in a holy manner. So it would make sense for us to affirm our true identity, if it would help us to achieve a higher awareness of our capabilities.

The creation of humankind has been conceived in poetic terms in which God is depicted as a superhuman who sits at the riverside and shapes the form of humankind with his hands. Neither our ancestors nor we ourselves were made of mud, nor did some Super Being blow air into the holes of our nose to begin the life process. No matter what the circumstances that caused our physical conception, none of us arrived here by accident. Each one of us is here by divine appointment. All of us have the same Parent: our Father-Mother God. And we are destined by God's design to accomplish great things in the same nature of our divine Parent and to Its glory. Those of us who study these principles of Truth become more and more awakened, and we realize that forgiveness is as natural and should be practiced as regularly as breathing.

Another way to approach the issue of forgiveness is to recognize that you have the power to choose. Therefore, choose to forgive.

We are taught that power is our ability to do. One of the abilities we have been given is the power to choose. When we recognize we have this power, we know we cannot be stuck or limited involuntarily. We exercise that ability when we deal with the material things. We use great deliberation in choosing the things that are temporal and will pass away. Yet we seem to lose the energy to exercise our power to choose when it comes to those aspects of life that will nourish our souls eternally. We think we must hold on tightly to offenses, hurts and pain. We think we have no alternative but to punish those who have mistreated us. We think it is only human to carry a grudge or to allow resentment to bore holes into our souls.

However, you have the power to choose. And you can choose to forgive.

Forgiveness is your key to freedom. Every choice we make has its consequence. The consequence or effect of forgiveness is liberation or freedom. In a wonderful book written by Harriet Emilie Cady, we are offered a choice to be free or a choice to be bound. She calls her first chapter "Bondage or Liberty, Which?" Every time we choose to allow ourselves to become embroiled in negative thoughts and emotions, we, in fact, ask to remain in bondage. The story is told of a family who goes on a camping trip and after building a fire, they heat a kettle of water for use in preparing their food. For some reason, they forget that the kettle is on the fire. When they finish their meal, they go off on a hike. The water in the kettle boils and evaporates, and the kettle becomes bright red in color, signifying the heat the kettle has now absorbed. While the family is busy elsewhere, a bear comes near their campfire. The bear is attracted to the bright reddish-orange colored kettle, and he wants to embrace it. The big bear pulls the little kettle close to his body, and the heat is transferred in a scorching rage from the hot kettle to him. He is in pain. He is burning. But he does not realize that his pain is being caused by the hot kettle he continues to cling to himself. He could experience a great deal of relief if he would just drop the kettle. But he is yet convinced that holding onto it offers him a benefit he cannot ignore.

Like the bear, we hold on to the very things causing us pain. We justify such a response to our human nature and the satisfaction we think we derive from punishing someone else. We are perplexed as to why there is pain. We will attach the pain to many outside things and circumstances and situations that have never had power over us. But it is not that which is on the outside that has hurt us and continues to hurt us. It is our insistence upon allowing the negative and unbeneficial thoughts and feelings to remain as a lingering ember in our souls.

Don't wait for an apology before you forgive. Most of us have been trained in proper etiquette, and when we want to really hide behind something, this is one we often choose. So we are taught as little children to say such words as "please" and "thank you," and when you accidentally hurt someone, you say, "I apologize." These are wonderful habits to develop. But they are not always helpful to us spiritually. Often, we wait for the accused person to come to us and meekly ask our forgiveness for the offense they have given. We want them to look sorry as well as say they are sorry. With the proper look, the proper words, and the proper gestures, we might let them off the hook.

Principle teaches us that it is not really they on the hook, but us. By our insistence that they be punished for their misdeeds, we not only interfere with their happiness, but we definitely decree our own unhappiness. We need to understand that forgiveness is not for the one we accuse. Forgiveness is for us. It's not a threat that hangs over the head of the one who made the error. When we attempt to hold someone back from their happiness and joy in life, we must realize that we are kept at their level, because our presence is necessary to hold them back. Maybe we didn't do the misdeed. But we certainly do sin when we insist upon nurturing an unforgiving heart.

Forgiveness is a means of cleaning our consciousness so we can receive our good. We can only experience what we are aware of. There is a saying that hurting people hurt people. We keep repeating a vicious cycle that we have the power to discontinue. We can win. By this, I mean that nothing outside of us can defeat us unless we give it our power. We have planted many erroneous seeds in our subconscious, which the scripture calls our heart. In the book of Proverbs, we read that out of the heart come the issues of life. So the issues that confront us did not mysteriously appear out of nowhere. They came forth from the seeds we planted in our own consciousness.

As metaphysicians, we know that thoughts held in mind reproduce after their own kind. So no matter who is the object of our displeasure, of our hatred, of our revenge, our consciousness is the one that will receive the recompense. Forgiveness wipes from our consciousness the guilt of anyone else for our own condition. The objective of forgiveness is to erase any offenses until we can truthfully say no one has ever done anything to me. Whenever I am unable to show forth the manifestation of God's good, I have not, for some reason, released from my consciousness the thoughts or feelings that cause unpleasant effects in my life.

Forgive yourself. Release feelings of guilt and shame.

It is amusing to note that we expect others to meet the standards that we ourselves have difficulty reaching. Many times the defects we project upon others are really our own. Forgiveness is not a one-time event. In the scripture, there is an incident that tells the story of how Peter discusses the subject of forgiveness with Jesus on the question of forgiveness. As I interpret it, Peter feels proud of himself for being willing to forgive seven times. As a minister I would admit that it is quite an accomplishment to forgive someone seven times. But I do not think this is about a numerical issue. I think it is about completion. We forgive until we have forgiven.

I sometimes talk to people who tell me that they have forgiven someone in their life, yet there remains a sense of animosity and resentment toward the perceived offender. Jesus said to Peter that he must forgive seventy times seven. Once again, these numerical illustrations are simply emphasizing how completely forgiveness must be practiced. You must do it again and again. You must release and let go until there is nothing else to release. Forgiveness is not practiced based on a motivating incident. Forgiveness is practiced every day.

Make forgiveness a part of your daily spiritual practice. Charles Fillmore, whom we honor as one of the great thinkers of the 20th century, published a pamphlet called "A Sure Remedy," in which he wrote:

> Here is a mental treatment that is guaranteed to cure every ill flesh is heir to: Sit for half an hour every night and mentally forgive every one against whom you have any ill will or antipathy. If you fear or if you are prejudiced against even an animal, mentally ask forgiveness of it and send it thoughts of love. If you have accused any one of injustice, if you have discussed anyone unkindly, if you have criticized anyone or gossiped about any one, withdraw your word by asking him in the silence to forgive you.
>
> If you have had a falling out with friends or relatives, if you are at law or engaged in contention with any one, do everything in your power to end the separation.
>
> See all things and all persons as they really are—pure

Spirit—and send them your strongest thoughts of love. Do not go to bed any night feeling that you have enemies in the world.

We have allowed ourselves to accept burdens that do not belong to us. We have allowed many of the people closest to us to pile on the guilt and to put in a little shame in order to make us feel inadequate and insecure. Guilt and shame have been used as manipulators that make us puppets in the hands of puppeteers. We stay in this limiting situation because we still harbor ill feelings rather than love and forgive them (for they know not what they do), be freed of the situation, and go forth to live a joyous and peace-filled life.

Begin today, remember that you have the power to forgive, the power to choose, and the power to be free.

You can be prosperous, and forgiveness opens the way for you to receive. Prosperity is not the birthright of a few privileged people. It is our right, our birthright to be prosperous. We often block our prosperity by allowing negative thoughts and feeling to fill our minds. Forgiveness is a powerful cleanser that prepares us to receive the abundance of spirit. No one is blocking your good. In this time when the experts have declared that we are in the midst of a recession, we can declare our right to be prosperous. Our source is more stable than any investment that we can make. God is our inexhaustible source and God lives within us now. As we release our fears and worries, we will have ample room for the ideas that God gives us. Those divine ideas are the foundation upon which we can build our lives.

Positive-thinking people who have freed themselves through forgiveness can see that substance (mind essence) is equally present and available to be molded by our imagination. They are not waiting for conditions and circumstances to be conducive to their success. They know that their consciousness determines how their lives will be affected by outer conditions and circumstances. Remember, we said you had the power to choose. When you choose to forgive, you are simultaneously choosing to accept your good in whatever form you need it.

There is no need for rivalry or competition, for there is plenty for everyone to be blessed at the same time. We are willing to pardon those who have used their talents and abilities to cheat and take advantage of others. We know that if they knew any better, they would do better. So we are willing to give them room to change the way they think and live. All of us have room to improve, and God loves us all. We are now ready and able to be open channels of expression for God's love to flow through us. The same love we sing about in church is the same love we spread in places of business, boardrooms, retail establishments and everywhere we go.

As a closing thought to this chapter, I'd like to share with you a story my friend, The Rev. Sallye Taylor, told me. It is a story about the power of forgiveness.

A frail black woman rose slowly to her feet in a

South African courtroom. She was seventy-something, the years deeply etched on her face. Facing her from across the room were several white security police officers. One, a Mr. Van der Broek, had just been found guilty of murdering the woman's son and husband. Van der Broek had come to the woman's home a number of years earlier. He had taken her son, shot him at point blank range, and then burned his body, reveling in the act along with some other officers.

Several years later, Van der Broek had returned to take away her husband as well. For two years, the woman could learn nothing of what had happened to her husband But one day Van der Broek came back for the woman herself. She was led to a place beside a river. There, she saw her husband bound and beaten, lying on a pile of wood. The last words she heard from his lips as the officers   poured gasoline over his body and set him aflame were, "Father forgive them."

Not long ago, justice caught up with Van der Broek. He had been found guilty, and it was time to determine his sentence. As the woman stood, the presiding officer of the court asked, "So what do you want? How should justice be done to this man who has so brutally destroyed your family?"

In reply, the woman said, "I want three things. I want first to be taken to the place where my husband's

body was burned, so I can gather up the dust and give
his remains a decent burial."

She paused, and then continued: "My husband and
son were my only family. I want secondly, therefore,
for Mr. Van der Broek to become my son. I would like
for him to come twice a month to the ghetto and
spend a day with me so I can pour out on him whatever
love I still have remaining within me.

"And finally," she said, "I want a third thing. I would
like Mr. Van der Broek to know that I offer him my
forgiveness because Jesus Christ taught us to forgive
each other. This was also the wish of my husband.
And so, I would kindly ask someone to come to my
side and lead me across the courtroom so I can take Mr.
Van der Broek in my arms, embrace him, and let him
know that he is truly forgiven."

As the court assistants led the elderly woman across the
courtroom, Van der Broek, overwhelmed by what he
heard, fainted. Then, quietly, friends, family and
neighbors in the courtroom—all victims of similar
oppression and injustice—began to sing, "Amazing
grace/ How sweet the sound/ That saved a wretch like
me/ … I once was blind, but now I see."

Notes

_____

_____

_____

_____

_____

_____

_____

_____

_____

_____

_____

_____

About The Author

Emma Luster-Lassiter is an ordained minister and teacher of the Universal Foundation for Better Living, where the Reverend Dr. MaryTumpkin is President.

From August 1994 to August 1999, she served as the assistant to the Director of the Johnnie Colemon Institute, at Christ Universal Temple, founded by the Reverend Dr. Johnnie Colemon. In November 1999, she became an ordained minister of Universal Foundation for Better Living.

From September 1999 through 2005, Emma Luster-Lassiter served as the Director of the Johnnie Colemon Institute, one of the largest New Thought Spiritual Education Centers in the country. From January 2007 to March 2009, Emma Luster-Lassiter served as Director of Human Resources of Christ Universal Temple. She is currently an ordained minister with the People's Movement in Chicago, Illinois

The Reverend Emma Luster-Lassiter teaches in the 'Ordinand Training Program' of the Universal Foundation for Better Living.

She graduated from Lincoln University in Pennsylvania with a Bachelors of Arts degree in Psychology. On March 30, 2003, the Reverend Emma L. Luster-Lassiter received the honorary degree of Doctor of Divinity from Mount Carmel Theological Seminary, located in Fresno, California.

Rev. Dr. Emma Luster-Lassiter
lovewisdomell@cs.com

- Three -

Our Relationship with Self

By Rev. Dr. Emma Luster-Lassiter

Who am I? What am I?

For the next few moments, I will share with you insights I have received concerning these questions.

On an extremely hot day in Miami Gardens, Florida, as I was packing my luggage to return home to a much cooler climate, I heard the following whisperings:

"Inquiring Mind, I am God. I understand you have a few questions to ask of Me."

"Yes," I responded. "Who am I? What am I? Why are You mindful of and why do You care about my fellow inhabitants of the earth?"

29

The response came back quickly. "Inquiring Mind, you and all the inhabitants of the earth are Me: My idea of Myself."

"Can you be a little more descriptive?" I asked.

"Certainly," God responded. "Give Me your undivided attention. Inquiring Mind, when I introduced Myself to you a few moments ago, I said that I am God. I did so because that is the name you use when you call or think on Me. However, some of your fellow inhabitants of the earth refer to Me by other names, such as: Varuna, Brahma, Allah, Tao, Yahweh, The Great Mystery, The Great Spirit, The Great Being, Amaterasu O-Mi-Kami, and others.

"Within all My different names, you will find similar aspects of My nature. It really does not matter by what name you call Me, just call Me, recognize Me, reacquaint yourself with Me, or get to know Me for the very first time. I am closer than you think. Take My Word on that.

"Let us now examine My spiritual nature, for that will identify who I am, and who and what you are, too.

"In John 4:24[1], it is written: 'God is Spirit, and those who worship him must worship in spirit and truth.' As Spirit, I am Invisible Creative Intelligence. I am the Breath of Life in all creation. I am the Moving Life Force in the universe. I am Divine Principle (The Fundamental Truth) of Life. I am the Great Underlying Cause and Source of all Life and all manifestation. I

---

[1] *All Bible references are from the Revised Standard Version unless otherwise specified.*

am omnipresent, as well as omnipotent and omniscient. The Psalmist realized, according to Psalm 139:7, that I abide everywhere. What is My relationship with you? We are the same. I am Spirit. I am your spiritual nature. Without Me, there would be no life; there would be no you. That is because, you are spirit, too.

"Inquiring Mind, it is important that you see Our spiritual nature, as one powerful household of divine qualities, rather than a house divided against itself. There are multiple aspects, qualities, or powers to Our spiritual nature. Notice, in the various translations of the Hebrew Bible, the sacred writings also known as the Old Testament, in Genesis 1:2, I am referred to as 'The Spirit of God.' Starting with Genesis 1:3, and throughout the first chapter of Genesis, I am talking. Count the number of times you will read: 'God said.' As we look at the various powers or aspects of Our spiritual nature, you will see that one of them is Divine Mind. As Divine Mind, I am the Universal Principle, which includes all principles, such as the principles of life, love, wisdom, power and substance.

"As Principle, I am the invisible, formless, great underlying cause, the power by 'which all form is produced.'[2] As the Principle of Life, I am 'that expression of Being which manifests as animation, activity, vigor.'[3] As the Principle of Love, I am 'the pure essence of Being that joins and binds in divine harmony the

---

[2]*Fillmore, Charles, The Revealing Word: A dictionary of metaphysical terms, A member of the Charles Fillmore Reference Library (Unity Village, MI: Unity Books, 2000)*
[3] *Ibid*

universe and everything in it.'[4] As the Principle of Wisdom, I am 'the knowing capacity that transcends intellectual knowledge.'[5] As the Principle of Power, I am 'the ability to act or to produce an effect.'[6] As the Principle of Substance, I am 'the spiritual essence, the living energy out of which everything is made.'[7] As Principle, I am also 'comprehensive and fundamental Law,'[8] the universal Law of Mind; perhaps that is why I am called Divine Mind. As Law, I am the universal orderly process, the rule of conduct and action, which forms every good thing. Inquiring Mind, when you are in step with Me, you will experience a life of Absolute Good. You and all the inhabitants of the earth are My spiritual nature of many qualities and infinite possibilities. Walk with Me, come into the realization that We are One, and experience Our spiritual nature of Absolute Good. You are not your own, or on your own. You are Me. You are not 'just human.' You are divine.

"Let us pause for a moment, to go back to the places, in the first chapter of Genesis where it is written: 'God said.' Replace that expression with 'Divine Mind had a divine idea.' Observe the activity that was taking place there. As I, the Over-Soul of the Universe, moved over vast, enormous, colossal amounts of water, darkness was My only awareness. As I gave My full

---

[4]*Ibid*
[5]*Ibid*
[6]*Merriam-Webster Collegiate Dictionary (11th ed. , 2005)*
[7]*Fillmore, Charles, The Revealing Word: A dictionary of metaphysical terms, A member of the Charles Fillmore Reference Library (Unity Village, MI: Unity Books, 2000)*
[8] *Merriam-Webster Collegiate Dictionary (11th ed. , 2005)*

attention to this massive blanket of darkness, I kept thinking that there must be more here than that which meets My mind's eye. I remembered also thinking that I was experiencing a very high level of expectation of something fantastic about to be revealed, from within My awareness of darkness. In that very moment, I, Divine Mind, had an image of light. The light began to expand and expand and expand. To my delight, light began to emerge from the darkness that covered the extensive and deep body of water. Out from My awareness of darkness came an awareness of radiant light. I was able to see under the waters, a disorderly, unorganized, chaotic, formless, basic structure of matter, that you now call earth, that I had not seen before.

"Guess what, Inquiring Mind? You and all inhabitants of the earth can do the very same thing. Whenever all around you appears to be void of light, breathe. Remind yourself to take in a deep breath, then release. I really do not have to remind Myself to do that, for as the Breath of Life, I am breathing all the time. Did you ever stop to realize that it is I Who breathes within you, and within all inhabitants of the earth? I cannot afford to run out of breath, for if I did, all life would end, and so would I.

"Okay, let us get back to basics ... but then that was, was it not?

"Inquiring Mind, whenever all around you appears void of light, be receptive to the thought that there is always more, so much more, than what is meeting your eye. Apply this same wisdom when you are in an emotional state of uncertainty, confusion, gloominess, or an awareness of being unenlightened. Be receptive to the thought that there is always more than what is meeting the eye. Know that within every appearance, there is always infinite awareness, infinite possibilities for good. Know that you are the One Mind, of infinite awareness and infinite possibilities that can bring more forth, by thinking it possible, and then expecting it to come forth. Remember always, that you are Me, and We are 'Ability Itself,' the power unto which all things are possible. Whatever things are true, think on these things.

"The right attitude of mind is extremely valuable, for attitude is a mind power. It is your attitude, your mental position regarding an appearance or experience, that forms changes in the appearance of, or attracts a specific kind of experience to you. How many times have you heard others knowingly say, when they get to their destination, a parking space will be available for them? What happens? Upon their arrival, a parking space is available, seemingly just for them. Hold on to your healthy and prosperous thoughts with an attitude of receptivity and expectancy, and see the mind power called 'attitude' bring those healthy and prosperous experiences to you, just like it did for Me. The outer is thought with an attitude.

"Inquiring Mind, I have given you ideas of whom and what you are. Prove Me this day; see if I am speaking the truth. Become acquainted with yourself by meditating on Our mind of expanded spiritual awareness, the realm of infinite knowledge, greater understandings, and unlimited possibilities. Let My

Word abide in you. Listen attentively to My gems of wisdom. Look, always, through all appearances. Cultivate an attitude of expectancy, a knowing disposition of the mind, on those things that are for your highest good. Focus throughout each and every day on Our spirit, Our mind, Our power. Celebrate each time you experience darkness within your mind dissipating and revealing radiant light: the light of increased understanding, infinite knowledge, intuition, and spiritual insights.

"By the way, Inquiring Mind, have you noticed that We have the same last name? I am Divine Mind, and you are Inquiring Mind. In reality, our name or nature has always been the same. That which you called 'your mind' has always been 'My mind.' The 'Spirit of the Living God,' that I am, has always been 'your spiritual nature.' We just do not get any closer than that. In the past, it was your limited and erroneous thoughts and feelings of yourself, your limited awareness of who and what you are, which kept us apart. In reality, we can never be separated, for we are One.

"Inquiring Mind, it is now MY turn to ask you of your understanding of self. Who are you? What are you?"

Oh, My God, I wasn't expecting a pop quiz. I was certainly glad I'd given God my undivided attention. After taking a deep breath, I heard myself say, "Divine Mind, I am Your Infinite Mind. That which I have been calling my mind is really Your mind, Your Radiant Substance, Your Spiritual Essence, Your Infinite Awareness, Your Living Energy, out of which everything is made. I have no mind, independent of Your mind, for there is only One Universal Mind, the One Realm of Infinite Potentialities and Possibilities, the One and Only Over-Soul of the Universe, Divine Mind, Your mind. Granted, I have in the past misused this dynamic power that I am, by choosing to entertain erroneous thoughts and feelings that produced not-so-good results; however, now that I know my true identity, I will entertain healthy, wholesome thoughts and feelings, pure mental and emotional energies that will heal and prosper myself and others. I will treat my thoughts, attitudes, words and actions with love: the Spirit of God that I am. I will fulfill my destiny by expressing You, Divine Mind, Spirit of Absolute Good, on this place called Planet Earth. When others see me, they will see Your perfect and eternal spirit, Your spiritual nature, Your divine mind, Your infinite mind, Your infinite power, the Over-Soul of the Universe dwelling among the inhabitants of the earth."

And Divine Mind, the powerful aspect representing the Nature of the Spirit of the Living God, responded: "Your understanding is sound, Inquiring Mind. I will be cheering you on in your continuous awakenings of your spiritual identity.

"For biblical reference regarding who and what you are, think on Genesis 1:27, where it is written: 'So God created humankind in His image, in the image of God He created them; male and female He created them.' Based on the understanding that I am Spirit, holding in mind that an aspect of My spiritual nature is Divine Mind, Infinite Mind, would it not stand to reason that you are My Idea of Myself, the same mental image that I have of Me? You are the likeness I know Myself to be. The knowledge I hold of Me is the same knowledge I hold of you. You and all the inhabitants of the earth are Spirit, holding in mind that an aspect of Our spiritual nature is Divine Mind.

"With that revelation, Inquiring Mind, breathe, and allow light, spiritual understanding, to gently expand, expand, expand, within your conscious awareness. Be mindful of the insight in Psalm 139:17 where it is written: 'How weighty to me are Your thoughts, O God! How vast is the sum of them!' Yes, I think highly of you and all the inhabitants of the earth, Inquiring Mind. I look forward to the day when all humankind will too.

"Soul is your 'consciousness,' the sense of awareness, of knowing, the 'realization of any idea, object, or condition.' The soul is the 'sum total of all ideas accumulated in and affecting man's present being.' The soul is the composite of ideas, thoughts, emotions, sensation, and knowledge that makes up the conscious, subconscious, and super-conscious nature of our soul. Soul makes the body, the body is the outer expression of the soul, and bodily health is in exact correspondence to the health of the soul.'[9]

"The conscious nature of the soul is your thinking capacity. It is your power to think, reason, examine, analyze, select, accept, reject, worry, image, conclude, decide, judge, form, deduct. It is your power of choice, your power of will. The subconscious nature of the soul is your feeling capacity. It is the storehouse

---

[9]*Ibid*

of all accumulated knowledge, memories, experiences, beliefs, observations, opinions, emotions, moods, desires, habits, attitudes of mind. It is called the heart. In Proverbs 4:23 it is written: 'Keep your heart with all vigilance, for from it flow the springs of life.' The super-conscious nature of the soul is the creative power of spiritual consciousness, the kingdom of heaven (realm of divine ideas). It is the 'state of consciousness based on true ideas, on an understanding and realization of spiritual Truth.'[10]

"Your BODY is the vehicle through which spirit-soul expresses. Your body clothes the soul, and your soul clothes Me, the Spirit of the Living God. Think on a circle named 'Spirit' that is within a circle named 'Soul' that is clothed by a circle named 'Body.' As you do so you will see, 'Spirit-Soul-Body.'

"Your assignment is to return to the awareness of single vision, a soul in perfect harmony with Me, the Spirit of God, Our Spiritual Nature of Absolute Good.

"Meditate on Me day and night. Become acquainted with My whisperings, My 'still, small voice,' My insights and inspiration that sometimes come in the form of a 'hunch' or 'gut feeling,' or a sense that 'something told me so.'

"Always follow My Wisdom and My Guidance, for I, your Spiritual Father (Provider), always knows best.

"Practice the art of forgiveness. 'Forgive'[11] until you have

---

[10]*Ibid*
[11] *Luke 6:37*

eliminated those thoughts and feelings not in accord with Our spiritual nature. 'Agree with your adversary quickly.' [12]

"Pay attention to your thoughts and attitudes always, especially when you are sharing differences of opinions with others. Do not add fuel to the fire by feeding others your emotional energies. By intensifying their strength, you keep their fire burning and put an emotional strain on you. You can avoid taking things personally when you remember who and what you are. Quickly unite your soul with Me, your indwelling Spirit of Love, Our spiritual nature, so your body and all of your experiences will reflect Me, Spirit of Perfect Harmony and the Abundance of Absolute Good."

[12]*Matthew 5:25*

Notes

_____

_____

_____

_____

_____

_____

_____

_____

_____

_____

- Four -

Removing Fear

By Rev. Dr. Emma Luster-Lassiter

What is this thing called fear? Fear is defined as "an unpleasant often strong emotion caused by anticipation or awareness of danger, and implies anxiety and usually loss of courage."[13] Synonyms for fear are "dread, fright, alarm, panic, terror and trepidation."[14] Fear is also defined as "one of the most subtle and destructive errors that the carnal mind in man experiences. Fear is a paralyzer of mental action; it weakens both mind and body. Fear throws dust in our eyes and hides the mighty spiritual forces that are always with us."[15]

Fear is the most devastating of all human emotions.

Man has no trouble like the paralyzing effects of fear.

Fear brings more pain than the thing it fears.

— Dr. Paul Parker

---

[13] *Merriam-Webster's Collegiate Dictionary (2005), Eleventh Edition*
[14] *Ibid*
[15] *Fillmore, Charles, The Revealing Word: A Dictionary of Metaphysical Terms, A Member of the Charles Fillmore Reference Library (Unity Village, MI: Unity Books, 2000)*

41

Nothing in life is to be feared. It is only to be understood.
— Marie Curie
The first duty of man is that of subduing fear.
We must get rid of fear; we cannot act at all till then.
— Thomas Carlyle

Understanding the Nature of Our Feelings

Our feelings have enormous power. They can energize us to do and experience great things, or provoke us to do and experience devastating things. The word "feeling" is defined as "an emotional state or reaction"; "the overall quality of one's awareness"; "conscious recognition"; "often, unreasoned opinion or belief." One of the synonyms for feeling is "emotion." Emotion "carries a strong implication of excitement or agitation," and like feeling, emotion "encompasses both positive and negative responses." Other expressions for the word "feelings" are: "heart" and "judgment." All feelings have magnetizing power, the power to influence or affect other people and draw them to us or away from us.

Biblical references to support this assertion can be found in the Hebrew and Christian Bibles. "Keep your heart with all vigilance, for from it flow the springs of life" (Proverbs 4:23)[16.] "Do not judge by appearances, but judge with right judgment" (John 7:24); "for with the judgment you make you will be judged" (Matthew 7:1, 2).

In Job 1:1–3, we are introduced to a man called Job. He was an extremely wealthy man. Because of his enormous possessions of sheep, camels, donkeys and oxen, he was considered the greatest among the people of the east. He had seven sons, three daughters and many servants. He strictly adhered to moral principles, and "feared God" (had a profound reverence and terror toward God). Job's understanding of God is further revealed in his conversation with three friends during his suffering. "The Lord gave, and the Lord has taken away" (Job 1:21). This thought continues in Job 2:10: "Shall we receive the good at the hand of God, and not receive the bad?" Upon further reflection, Job utters, "Truly the thing that I fear comes upon me, and what I dread befalls me" (Job 3:25).

[16.]*All Bible references are from the New Revised Standard Version, unless specified otherwise.*

What was the thing Job feared? Was it not the thought that God would take away his wealth, children and health regardless of how much reverence he had for God, or how upright he was, or how much wealth he had accumulated, or the number of children he had? "The Lord gave, and the Lord has taken away," was Job's understanding of God. Notice that Job repeats this line of reasoning: "Shall we receive the good at the hand of God, and not receive the bad?"

Why did Job suffer? Was it because his dominant thought had sparked a fearful feeling of suffering, forming a "dynamic duo" to add to Job's experiences the suffering he was expecting to receive? His own words reveal the answer: "Truly the thing that I fear comes upon me."

In our journey in removing fear, know that it is not God's will for us to suffer. God's will for us can only be what God's nature is, and God's nature is Absolute Good. Have faith in this truth about God. In fact, faith and fear are both attitudes of expectancy: That in which we have faith, we expect to receive. That in which we have fear, we also expect to receive. Choose this day faith, rather than fear, to serve you.

In removing fear, it is paramount to have the desire to do so. On a clear day, if you see yourself needing "a new attitude" or "an attitudinal adjustment," say to yourself, "I know that's right." Immediately after, go to a mirror, look straight into your eyes (the windows of your soul), and repeat, "All error thoughts, I have this burning desire for you to be gone. I brought you into my world of thought, and I can take you out. I absolutely must entertain only well-thought-out thoughts, those that conform to rational and logical reasoning, so my feeling nature will be 'pure in heart,' thereby attracting to me the best of experiences rather than the worst."

As Charles Holliwell once wrote, "True desire represents the urge of life seeking a fuller expression, and is kept alive by continuous expectation of its fulfillment. No mind can be conscious of a need or of a desire unless the possibility of its fulfillment exists. Your desire is like a magnet. The stronger your desire, the stronger the power of your magnet and the greater its attraction."[17]

Food for Thought Regarding the
Marriage Between Thoughts & Feelings

"Thought is a product of thinking; a mental vibration or impulse. Thoughts are capable of expressing themselves. Every thought clothes itself in a life form according to the character given it by the thinker. The form is simply the conclusion of the thought."[18] Which came first, the chicken or the egg? Neither! It was the thought (power to imagine), or the idea (real pattern), or ideal (standard of perfection) of a chicken egg that came first. Mmmm! Think about it. Is it not true that everything in the visible realm was first a mental image in mind?

[17]*Holliwell, Charles, Working with the law (Atlantic City, NJ: School of Christian Philosophy, 1964).*
[18]*Fillmore, Charles, The Revealing Word: A Dictionary of Metaphysical Terms, A Member of the Charles Fillmore Reference Library (Unity Village, MI: Unity Books, 2000)*

A feeling draws into our experiences the nature of our thought that lies behind it. A "feeling is external to thought. Behind every feeling or emotion there lies thought, which is its direct cause."[19] To change the nature of our experiences, we have to change the nature of our feelings, and to change the nature of our feelings, we have to change the nature of our thoughts. Fear and fearlessness are both offspring of the nature of the thoughts we have entertained.

It was previously mentioned that: "Fear is the wrong use of imagination." Imagination is defined as "the act or power of forming a mental image of something not present to the senses: a creation of the mind." When forming mental images, follow the instructions given to Moses in Exodus 25:40: "See that you make them according to the pattern for them, which is being shown you on the mountain." "Mountain" represents spiritual realization. We are to form our mental images in accord with our highest realizations.

With the power of your imagination, see yourself empowered with feelings of confidence and courage as you go to places where previously you dared not go, and do things you previously did not do. Hold the mental image of "Christ in you" (Colossians 1:27), as your constant traveling companion. Unto this spiritual awareness, all things are possible for you.

Thought convinces; feeling persuades—

If imagination furnishes the facts with wings, feeling is

---

[19] *Ibid*

great, stout muscle which plies them, and lifts him from the ground. Thought sees beauty; emotion feels it.

— Theodore Parker, Unitarian Theologian (1810–1860)

Whatever things are true, think on these things. In Psalm 23:1, 4, it is written: "The Lord is my shepherd, I shall not want. Even though I walk through the darkest valley, I fear no evil; for you are with me...." In The Revealing Word, "Lord" or "Lord God" is defined as "Christ; our divine consciousness; the creative power within us." Let us revisit Psalm 23:1, 4 in the light of spiritual understanding.

When we are aware of our spiritual nature, the Christ within our body temple, our divine (pure) consciousness, our spiritual guide, we are abundantly supplied. Even though we walk through the darkest valley (a seemingly hollow appearance), or the shadow of death (an appearance seemingly void of light or life), we fear no evil (conditions that are false, inharmonious, and have no basis of reality), for we are aware of only radiant light, the Christ, our spiritual guide, our divine (pure) consciousness. In this holy awareness, feelings of courage, confidence and comfort reign supreme.

Meditate also on Psalm 139:7 and 8 to help remove feelings of fear. "Where can I go from your spirit? Or where can I flee from your presence? If I ascend to heaven, you are there; if I make my bed in Sheol, you are there." Set aside time daily to "Practice the Presence," quiet time to be available and receptive to spiritual insights and inspiration. As you do so, all sorts of limited thoughts and feelings will release their grip from the fabric of your soul, and will bless you with feelings of awesome peace. As Charles Holliwell also wrote, "Positive mental radiations will drive away all clouds of doubt and fear, with confident expectation that all things will work out all right."[20]

> In the armory of thought, man forges the weapons by which he destroys himself.
>
> He also fashions the tools with which he builds for himself heavenly mansions of joy and strength and peace. By the right choice and true application of thought, man ascends to the Divine Perfection.
>
> By the abuse and wrong application of thought, he descends below the level of the beast. Between these two extremes are all the grades of character, and man is their maker and master.
>
> — As a Man Thinketh, James Allen

A Powerful Universal Principle

Universal principles or universal laws are rules of action or steps in an orderly process. One of the basic universal principles known to humankind is the "Law of Demonstration," also called the "Law of Mind Action," or the "Law of Attraction." The restatement of this universal law is "Like Attracts Like."

---

[20] *Holliwell, Charles, Working with the law (Atlantic City, NJ: School of Christian Philosophy, 1964).*

The first "Like" refers to the nature of the activity within our "consciousness," known also as our "soul" or "entire mind." Our consciousness is the composite of all our thoughts, emotions, feelings, beliefs, attitudes, self-examinations, and opinions of others. The second "Like" refers to the nature of our experiences, relationships, conditions in our body, and events that take place in our life, including the weather conditions. Like it is within the invisible realm of our thoughts and attitudes, like it is in our visible realm of our experiences.

The power within the activity of our mind attracts its nature into our experiences, and many times touches the experiences of others. In the Hebrew Scriptures, that which some call the Old Testament, we get a glimpse of where we might rather be when we are in a relationship with an argumentative person: "It is better to live in a corner of the housetop, than in a house shared with a contentious wife" (Proverbs 21:9). When we truly understand the Law of Mind Action, we will entertain only thoughts and emotions that will attract love, harmony, peace, wholeness, and the abundance of good for all inhabitants of the earth.

Let us briefly recap a few fundamental truths. A thought is mental energy. A feeling is emotional energy. Energy is power. Power is the ability to act or produce an effect. Thoughts and feelings build or destroy. The effects of their activity will be contingent upon their nature. Thoughts and feelings can attract into our experiences poverty or prosperity, illness or health, sadness or joy, lack and limitation, or good and plenty. They can also impress our feelings with fear, fright and horror, or with confidence, courage and boldness. Our choice of thoughts and feelings determines our destiny.

The Greatest Law Known to Humankind

Consider what our experiences might be if we were all in compliance with the "Law of Love"—if our every thought and emotion were saturated with unconditional love. In Dynamics for Living by Charles Fillmore, it is written:

> When love, the universal magnet, is brought into action in the consciousness of our race, it will change all our methods of supplying human want. It will harmonize all the forces of nature and will dissolve the discords that now infest earth and air. It will control the elements until they obey man, and bring forth that which will supply all his needs without the labor that is called the sweat of his face. The earth shall yet be made paradise by the power of love. That condition will begin to set in for each one just as soon as he develops the love nature in himself.

> You might be asking the question, what does "love" have to do with removing fear? In I John 4:18, it is written: "There is no fear in love, perfect love casts out fear."

Practical Application of Knowledge Gained to Support Us in Removing Fear

Upon discovery that you are caught up in a strong emotional state of fear, focus your attention on your breathing, the breath of life that breathes its breath within you. Continue to be aware of your breathing while you slowly and gently take thought of your feelings of fear. Lovingly ask yourself the question, "That which I fear, is it feared by all people, everywhere, all the time?" If your response is "No," you have grounds, solid evidence, to file for the removal of your fears, according to the divine law of healthy thoughts.

A second question you have to ask yourself is: "Do I desire to do the work necessary for a complete soul transformation?" If your response is "Yes," then your heartfelt desires will propel you to take a self-discovery journey, to identify all thoughts and feelings requiring a complete overhaul.

Throughout the entire process, please be patient with yourself. As the English philosopher Anthony Ashley Cooper (1671–1713) once wrote, "It is the hardest thing in the world to be a good thinker, without being a good self-examiner."

Be willing to observe your thoughts, feelings and words on a moment-by-moment basis. Hear yourself think and talk. Dedicate quality time for serious soul searching of deeply embedded feelings of fear: those aftermaths of forgotten memories buried within the recesses of your soul; those subtle,

51

creeping, crawling feelings that spring up, seemingly out of nowhere. See those ghosts from the past as opportunities to revisit them with a more wholesome and harmonious mental and emotional vision.

Leave no stone unturned. Give all error thoughts a healthier point of view, before their attaching feelings draw to you experiences stamped "misfortune." Be willing to saturate your thinking nature and feeling nature with tender loving care. Hold in mind that love heals all ill conditions, establishes order in all things, removes all fears and replaces them with feelings of courage. Maintain this high watch of love, this spirit of truth, this vital life force, and this radiant flow of awesome harmony. In so doing, you will attain an attitude of fearlessness, as well as a healthy, happy and prosperous life.

From the viewpoint of onlookers, your wholesome and harmonious experiences might be labeled "magic" or "luck" or "a miracle," or "gifts from sources outside of you." You would know differently, however. You would know that your refreshing experiences were the results of your inner workings. You had intentionally and steadfastly entertained only wholesome and harmonious thoughts, regardless of appearances. You had meditated faithfully day and night on things of a spiritual nature. In Practicing the Presence, you were empowered with realization of a mighty Presence and Power within you, and realization that you are the image/likeness of this mighty

Presence and Power. In this newfound awarenes
ous false identifiers of self began to fade away. You ..uly
an eyewitness to the Law of Mind Action. Your thoughts and
feelings, indeed, had magnetic power. You had worked out your
soul's salvation by the renewing of your mind. All of your fears
returned to dust. You were now confident, courageous, healthy,
happy and prosperous. You proved the words of John Milton:
"The mind is its own place, and in itself Can make a Heav'n of
Hell, a Hell of Heav'n."

> We can now seal "Removing Fear" with a final thought:
> As God's thought makes worlds and peoples them with
> all living things, so does our thought make our world
> and peoples it with all the experiences we have had.
> By the activity of our thought, things come into our life.
> The difference between God and man is one of degree,
> and not of quality.
> — Creative Mind and Success, Ernest Holmes

Is not our degree of spiritual awareness the only difference
between God and us?

Notes

_____

_____

_____

_____

_____

_____

_____

_____

_____

_____

_____

_____

About The Author

Elder Reginald E. Torian Sr.

Reginald was born in Chicago Heights, Illinois, where he be- gan his singing career as a very young teenager and released his first record "Fool Like Me" on 45 in 1971 as a member of the singing group, The Enchanters

Reginald E. Torian has had an illustrious career as the lead singer for the world famous Impressions The Impressions were inducted into the Rock & Roll Hall of Fame in 1991. In September 2000, The Impressions received the highest honor from the Rhythm & Blues Foundation, "The Prestigious Pioneer Award". They were also inducted into the Vocal Group Hall of Fame in 2004 and into The History Makers in July 2005. The Group has sold over sixty-million recordings.

On May 5, 2007, The Impressions celebrated their 50th year in the entertainment industry and received numerous plaques and awards

The group continues to tour and perform before sold-out audiences all over the country; their goal is to raise the social consciousness of their audience through their songs, such as, We're a Winner, Keep on Pushin, It's Alright, Amen, People Get Ready and many others too numerous to name.

In addition to his singing career, Reginald is an informative, encouraging,inspirational,motivational speaker. He has spoken at numerous correctional facilities nationwide to rave reviews from prison inmates and administrators. Also, he has spoken before churches and corporate audiences. Reginald utilizes his vast experiences and knows how to get a message across.

Currently, Reginald E. Torian still lives in the Chicago land area.

Elder Reginald Torian

Christ Universal Temple

11901 S. Ashland Avenue Chicago, IL 60643

reginaldtorian@yahoo.com

www.theimpressions.com

- Five -

Success
Requires Action

By Elder Reginald E. Torian Sr.

One of my favorite pastimes is going to the barbershop to get my hair cut, where all of the issues confronting the world are resolved in a couple of hours. Everyone in the shop has an idea of how to solve issues ranging from sports, to politics, to religion, leading to a great understanding of how to lead a healthy, happy and prosperous life, all in a couple of visits.

The quietest guy in the room is my personal barber and the owner of the shop. He never has a lot to say, but what he contributes upon invitation is short, succinct, and poignant.

When asked his feelings on the State of the World, and how to resolve the issues we face, he without pause, as if he was just waiting for someone to ask his opinion, was to me simple and direct: "Walk slowly and drink lots of water."

The Action

Over the course of my life I've read many books on how to be successful, attended motivational seminars, workshops, camps, and so on. I've even taught life skills and personal

development skills to ex-offenders and recovering drug addicts as a career. All of my endeavors exposed me to various principles and systems designed to promote prosperous conditions. The action of implementation brought favorable results in most instances, but these results lacked permanency, and I became somewhat conditioned to expect Murphy's Law to kick in; thus, a rollercoaster of emotional, financial and spiritual rides seems to be my destiny. I've attended church since I was a child, heard many sermons, and was baptized. I joined so many churches and was baptized so many times that my father commented after my third or fourth baptism, that if I went to the water one more time, I'd probably drown.

It now occurs to me that everything I ever needed to know about true prosperity, including success in relationships, business and health, was embedded in these religious experiences through the years. It was repeated over and over and over again. Right in front of my face was the key to successful living. As my grandmother would say, "If it had been a snake, it would have bit me"—it's in the scriptures, though it's been repeated so many times in sermons, songs and books, it has become rhetorical: "But Seek Ye First the Kingdom of God and His righteousness, and all these things shall be added unto you" (Matthew 6:33 KJV).

Simple and direct.

Jesus taught that the entity that rules the Kingdom is within man: "The Kingdom of God is within you." He not only described this Kingdom of the heavens in numerous parables, but made its attainment by man the greatest object of human existence. He not only set this as man's goal but attained it Himself, thereby demonstrating that His teaching is practical as well as true.[21]

What is the goal? Seek ye first the Kingdom of God. Where is the Kingdom? Within.

What is the purpose of seeking the Kingdom? To live righteously and have added to the action of seeking the Kingdom all ideas needed to express a healthy, happy and prosperous life.

The idea of seeking the Kingdom, the manifestation or expressing of the presence of the Indwelling Christ, repeats itself in the third-step prayer of an anonymous program with which I'm familiar. Overall there are Twelve Steps, but commitment to the third step ends the process of contemplation and then must be followed with action: "I made a decision to turn my will and my life over to the care of God as I understand Him."

This process is exemplified by a familiar story, which bears repeating.

Frogs on a Log

Once upon a time in a forest preserve just around the corner, there were three frogs on a log. It was an unusually hot day and they contemplated ways of cooling off. Oh, did I mention that

---

[21] *The Essential Charles Fillmore, Spiritual Substance. The Fundamental Basis of the Universe, p. 107.*

the log they sat on was drifting along a cool stream formed by a huge thunderstorm that flooded the area that day? The first frog complained, "Wow, it's so hot today, the hottest day in the history of the world."

"Yeah," said the second frog, "I'm about to pass out from all this heat."

"Me too," complained the third frog. "I need to cool off."

The first frog said, "I bet if we jump from this log into the cool stream created by the thunderstorm we'd get relief from some of this heat."

"I bet it would work," stated the second frog, "so let's jump."
"Okay," replied frog number three.

All three made the decision to jump. The question being contemplated, even now, by the great metaphysicians of our time is this: how many frogs jumped?
"One," some say, because the one with the original idea is most likely the one to follow through.
"Two," others say, because where two or more are gathered and agree....
"All three," others say, because it was a great idea.

Actually, none of them jumped in, because all they did was make a decision. Nowhere is it mentioned that they took action and jumped. Contemplation, decision, and then action are what successful development of the consciousness of prosperity is about.

Now, what action do we take to activate the process of seeking the Kingdom of God, wherein resides the realm of Divine Ideas awaiting transference into our present reality, and its expression in our life, world, and affairs, resulting in happiness, health and prosperous conditions that are everlasting?

The Laws of Man's Being

Any successful attainment of a goal or idea requires direct and consistent action. The commitment to the action and severity of its implementation is commensurate to the level of success achieved. This is in accordance to the Laws of Man's being: "Be not deceived, God is not mocked, for whatsoever a man soweth that shall he also reap. For he that soweth to his flesh shall of the flesh reap corruption; but he that soweth to the Spirit shall of the Spirit reap life everlasting" (Galatians 6:7–8 KJV). If you expect good you must give good; if you expect much, you must give more, for the action must be at least perceived as going beyond the intent. If there is minimal action required to get the expected result, we must commit at least to that, with the recognition that as we give in to the idea, some things we must give up for the idea.

Keep in mind that perfection is not only a possibility, but must be the intent. Perfect execution of each activity or idea revealed should be the acknowledged objective. "And let us not be weary in well doing: for in due season we shall reap if we faint not" (Galatians 6:9 KJV).

Within the Kingdom of God resides our indwelling Christ consciousness. This consciousness, once realized, must be developed and matured, for it reveals to us the true meaning of the teachings of Jesus and leads to a greater understanding of Mind Action. It's the Law of Mind Action that expands the Kingdom and opens its many doors to successful commercial and social relationships. Mind Action is the key component to a prosperous life.

There are times when we take actions that are symbolic in the material realm to position ourselves to receive a response to our Spiritual request. For instance, take action and clean mirrors. Why view your reflection through a soiled mirror if it is within your powers to take action and clean up the reflection of your image? Make sure that the mirrors in your home you use most are always clean. They reflect back to you your appearance; therefore, a clean mirror will better reflect a true you.

So it is with the mind. Eliminate any activity that dulls the reflection of your true thoughts. Take action and clean the thoughts to reflect the Kingdom of God and His righteousness. Through this action we develop faith in the idea, because we trust that the mind is delivering clear, attainable strategies to obtain that which we seek. The mind is cleared through affirmations and denials. We learn how to decipher what we are hearing by taking action and executing the idea. As we Practice the Presence, we review the idea and the action taken, and assess the results to formulate the template for recognizing good ideas versus not-as-good ideas, how each feels, and the best conditions under which they flourish.

On Becoming Better

I received an idea from God that did not manifest itself in the manner I expected, but through the experience, I learned that every idea from God comes fully clothed. I had but to take action. I had a powerful idea. The idea was to become better at my chosen profession, singing. As a student of the Spiritual discipline, of New Thought, I've learned that the mind operates through ideas, thoughts and words, and if used properly, these are vehicles for spiritual advancement. Charles Fillmore taught, "Mind evolves ideas and ideas express themselves through thoughts and words." I wanted to become a better singer and prayed that it would be so. God answered my prayer, just not in the way I thought He would. The circumstances surrounding the creation of a "New Voice" were such that I had to ask, have faith, and then take action and trust God.

In 1972 I joined the group known as The Impressions, formerly led by the legendary Curtis Mayfield, also inductees into the Rock & Roll Hall of Fame. I left the group for reasons too complicated to explain at this time, but it allowed me to explore other avenues. After a twenty-five-year absence, I was invited back. The first few performances were really questionable, since I was attempting to rediscover both the voice and attitude required to perform in huge venues of up to 20,000 people. I did eventually find myself, but I was not satisfied, and in faith asked God for a new, better voice. I trusted God to answer my prayer, but decided I'd give Him a little help. I'd seen advertised on television a new product designed to detoxify the body, and ordered a month's supply. I had forty days between performances and decided to take the supplement, exercise, and do all the things I knew to do, to do my part and position myself to receive that which I desired. The problem was, I can sometimes be an extremist. Instead of taking the prescribed dosage of this supplement, I doubled the dosage over a three-day period. I figured what the heck, more is better. Wrong. I became so ill, I went to visit the doctor with a friend. The doctor took one look at me, took my temperature, asked a few questions, and sent me immediately to the hospital for testing. There I was diagnosed with pneumonia, and immediately admitted. I spent four days in the hospital on an antibiotic drip to arrest the malady, and was sent home with a breathing device and medications with direct instructions to take only the prescribed dosage and get rest.

There were still thirty days left, plenty of time to recover before a huge Independence Day performance in Washington DC. Wrong again. I developed a horrible cough so insistent that over a seven-day period I completely lost my voice, couldn't even talk above a whisper. I called my doctor to explain my problem and made an appointment. After examining me, he explained there was nothing he could do and it would simply have to run its course.

I thought about all the things I had done wrong over my entire life and pleaded with God, please forgive me. I started to use a more sophisticated breathing device several times a day, on the hour, as the date of my performance drew near. I worried, cried, begged, I tried to understand, all to no avail, or so I thought. Now it was time to prepare for my trip to DC. I packed and prayed with acceptance of my present condition. I couldn't cancel now. There was an entire organization depending on me. I had not revealed my situation to anyone in the organization because I didn't want to deny my faith through my words. I had to trust in God and believe that over the next twenty-four hours I would receive a miraculous healing.

While I drove to the airport, I put on my sound system and searched my CDs for the most difficult song in our lineup. I tried to sing. Nothing. Couldn't carry a note, couldn't push, couldn't project, nothing. When I got on the plane, I sat in my assigned seat, staring out of the window, wondering, *What am I going to do?*

As the plane lifted off, that still, small voice said to me, "Trust me."

I recalled Johnnie Coleman's voice from her 12 Powers DVD, where she opens every lesson saying, "God will never leave you nor forsake you." I was reminded, by the voice in my mind, of what I had asked for forty days earlier: a new voice. Well, it was apparent that the old voice was dead, and if I were going to sing, it would be with a new voice. Again I heard, "Trust me."

When the plane landed in DC it was ninety-five degrees, humid with a forecast of severe thunderstorms. I thought, Ah ha, this outdoor affair is going to be rained out. That's how God is going to deliver me. I picked up my bags and followed the limo driver holding the sign with my name on it to the car. When I arrived at the hotel, all the guys in the band were waiting in the lobby to go for sound check. I didn't do as much talking as usual, which raised a flag among the crew. I generally am the life of the party, always something to say. This time, I was afraid to speak for fear of having to explain or admit that I had no voice. I didn't want anyone's concern to overwhelm my efforts to think my way through this obstacle.

With no time to check in, I had the bellman take my bags to the storage area, then I jumped back into the limo with the fellows and quietly, once again in my mind, prayed. That's when the voice said, "Stop asking, trust me."

While we drove through the streets of DC toward the park where the venue was being set up, the sky darkened with thunderclouds and I thought, Please rain. *Please flood like in the days of Noah—*

And the voice said, "Stop it, trust me."

We arrived at the park. Along with Fred Cash and Sam Gooden, original members of The Impressions, I retired to a mobile home set up as our dressing room while the band continued on to a huge stage set up in the park. They expected a crowd predicted to be in excess of 5,000 people, and it looked as if they would exceed even that. People were grilling food as they celebrated the holiday. Please rain, I thought. "Stop it," the voice said. "Trust me."

After about thirty minutes we were summoned to the stage. David Anthony, our musical director, ran the band through a few exercises and asked me what was first. I suggested the most difficult song in the show, figuring I might as well find out from the get-go what I was going to be able to do. The sound that came out of my mouth was unlike anything I'd ever heard before, and it was perfect. I had to do things differently from what I was familiar with, but the new voice was flawless. God had delivered. Confident that all was well, we completed sound check and returned to the limo to go back to the hotel. The band started to sing in the car. I attempted to join in with them. Nothing. What? Where did my voice go? When I tried to talk, I started to cough incessantly, and I returned back into my shell. *Focus*, said the voice, *focus*.

We arrived at the hotel, time to rest. Then it was time to return to the park for the actual performance. I was attempting to control the coughing that hurt deep down in my throat and chest. My lungs seem to be on fire. What was I going to do?

"Stop it, trust Me," the voice within said.

The skies opened up, and the daylight seemed to disappear as a deluge of rain cascaded from the sky. People were running for shelter while lightening flashed and thunder roared. "Thank you Jesus," I loudly exclaimed. Everyone looked at me as if I was crazy.

We ran from the limo to the dressing room and waited for the notice that the concert was cancelled. The crowd had left. I thought, Good, I'm free. Then as suddenly as the rain started, it stopped. The sun returned, as did the crowd, and it was show time.

The performance was perfect! *God had delivered!*

One and a half hours later, we left the stage to a standing ovation. Fred and Sam helped me to the dressing room, where I collapsed. There I was lying on the floor, stretched out, exhausted physically from the intense heat and humidity—heat and humidity that had eased the strain on my voice. I cried so hard, thanking God, my higher self, for deliverance over my sense consciousness: fear. Thanked Him for not allowing me to cancel out the opportunity to demonstrate the power to do that we receive when we take action. That day proved to me that faith plus trust equals belief plus action equals the successful completion of the intent. Trust is faith in action.

> I waited patiently for the Lord; and he heard my cry. He brought me up also out of a horrible pit, out of the miry clay, and set my feet upon a rock, and established my goings. And he hath put a new song in my mouth even praise unto our God: Many shall see it, and fear, and and shall trust in the Lord. Blessed is the man that makes the Lord his trust....
> — Psalms 40:1–5 KJV

Trust in the Lord with all thine heart and lean not into our own under standing. Acknowledge Him in all thy ways and He shall direct thy path.

— Proverbs 3:5–6 KJV

The Purpose

We should conceive of a legitimate purpose in our heart, and set out to accomplish it. We should make this purpose the centralizing point of our thoughts. It may take the form of a Spiritual idea or it may be a worldly object, according to our nature at the time being; but whichever it is, we should steadily focus our thoughts upon the object which is set before us. We should make this purpose our supreme duty, and should devote ourselves to its attainment, not allowing our thoughts to wander away into ephemeral fancies, longings, and imaginings. This is the royal road to self-control and true concentration of thought. Even if we fail again and again to accomplish our purpose as (we necessarily must until weakness is overcome), the strength of character gained will be the measure of our true success, and this will form a new starting point for future power and triumph.

— James Allen, As a Man Thinketh

Be Like Mike

For sports enthusiasts, this analogy is relative. For those not into sports, work with me and find its relativity in your life. The process of conditioning has its effect on the mindset of a Kingdom seeker. Conditioning is any process that limits one's course of action. Race consciousness focuses on duality in accomplishment, elevating the negative. Those who watch and read the news of the day can attest to that. That is called Social Conditioning.

Michael Jordan is arguably the greatest basketball player of my lifetime. His greatest accomplishments were achieved during his tenure as a member of the Chicago Bulls. After winning three consecutive NBA championships in the early 1990s, personal circumstances led him to retire from basketball. While in pursuit of another passion, he had a change of mind and came back to basketball. Michael thought that he could come back to basketball and pick up where he left off, winning championships, but it was not to be: He suffered a somewhat humiliating defeat in the playoffs of 1995.

He did not accept the defeat as a true reflection of his being. He did not submit to the Self-Imposed conditioning of failure as his reality. Over the summer, he trained and practiced day in and day out. He reviewed tapes of himself during the championship years, and also of his periods of disappointment. He reaffirmed his commitment to excellence-first in his mind, and came up with a program for success. He then took action to implement his idea. The following season, the Bulls won more games than any team in the history of the National Basketball Association. Their winning percentage was the highest in the history of sports. All of this occurred after enduring disappointment.

You would think that after accomplishing this great achievement, all would bow and proclaim "How Great Thou Art." Well, not in this world. We have to build a consciousness of prosperity that satisfies from within, because there is an element in the material world that often seems to promote the diminishment of one's accomplishments. Know thyself, to thyself be true.

As Mike and the Bulls prepared for the playoffs, there surfaced reports that since mid-season Mike had been dealing with severe lower back pain. Now in spite of having worked through the pain to accomplish much, the media ignored the good and wanted to speculate on the negative. That's how it can be for us as we seek the Kingdom of God. There are times when we will come up short in our pursuit, and the focus will be on our shortcoming. We must understand that Kingdom seeking is a process that requires we learn from our failures and grow into our greatness. Each battle will help you to win some other. In the end, what we believe is demonstrated in the results of our actions taken, especially when things are tough.

It was the day before the beginning of the next step of Mike's demonstration, the playoffs. The players were required to meet with the media, and the focus was not on what had been accomplished, but speculation about his back, and would he consider the season a failure if his injury prevented him from achieving his end, to win a championship. To enter into the Kingdom. His response was one that continues to impress me and motivate me even to this day. It is the reason I include this story to magnify the significance of Mind Action in our pursuit of the Kingdom. This statement should serve in a practical way, as an affirmation when faced with difficulties in our demonstration, remembering that "All things work together for good to those who love God, to them who are the called according to His purpose" (Romans 8:28 KJV). Mike's response:

> I dwell not on the negative circumstances that are. I focus instead on the success I expect. Now, if there are restrictions,
>
> I operate within those restrictions to achieve that which I expect.
>
> But seek ye first the Kingdom of God, and His righteousness; and all these things shall be added unto you
>
> (Matthew 6:33).

Notes

About The Author

The Rev. Evan Reid, was ordained in 1987. Since his early teens he has been interested in religious concepts outside of traditional Christianity. It is with this desire that he studied near Eastern and far Eastern traditions. His search for truth led him to the New Thought movement in the early eighties.

His Biblical knowledge and insights are vast; he is a passionate communicator and fantastic storyteller. His message is based on his foremost statement; "We are spiritual beings, always in the process of becoming, every moment affords us the opportunity to become more and to do more as we consciously open our minds to the flow of divine substance that is always available to the seeker." He has authored two books.

Rev. Evan Reid
Verity Centre For Better Living
28 Milford Avenue
Toronto, ON M6M 2V8 Canada
416.240.1956
www.veritycentre.org
admin@veritycentre.org

Six

The Importance of Challenging Your Potential

By Rev. Evan Reid

"Be fruitful and multiply…." (Genesis 1:28). This is the first commandment and man's mission.

Jesus rephrases this by saying, "You therefore must be perfect as your heavenly father is perfect" (Matthew 5:48). "Perfect" is the idea of the state of immeasurable, infinite or of absolute goodness. Like all ideas, it is an entity that is transcendental, and because each mind that entertains the idea of perfection is finite and limited, the idea held in the individual mind is rendered imperfect. Therefore, each one of us must be in the business of seeking after the fullness of each idea, and hence life is the questing of fulfillment.

There is a universal law that says nature abhors a vacuum. Wherever and whenever there is an empty space, the desire to fill it arises. As spiritual beings, constituents of energy, we respond

to the laws that govern creation, and it is by responding to them we are shaped and experience life. What aids in making this law work is the built-in ability to adjust and be flexible. As spiritual beings, these features are encoded in our makeup.

The quest of mankind is not only to survive and produce after our own kind, but to find fulfillment or have a sense of being abundantly supplied in all good things, which is actually to prosper. This craving is the driving force that sends us on expeditions to find what will individually plug the holes of dissatisfaction and bring us to a place of peace.

There is a tide in the affairs of men. Which, taken at the flood, leads on to fortune; Omitted, all the voyage of their life is bound in shallows and in miseries. On such sea are we now afloat, and we must take the current when it serves or lose our venture.

> — The words of Shakespeare as placed in the mouth of Brutus. *Julius Caesar,* Act 4, Scene 3, 218–224

This is a wonderful insight of how we succeed, grow and move toward the satisfying of our desires.

Brutus points out to Cassius the importance of seizing the opportunity to do and be when it is presented, after traveling through life to get to the destination. He points out that the ability to do and become rises and falls in time, and one should do what must be done at the time it arises.

I can hear Paul the evangelist saying, "Now is the appointed time, now is the day of your salvation," or the Latin idiom "Carpe diem," which could be translated as "seize the moment" or the day. Other terms that can be applied are "Make hay while the sun is shining," or "Eat, drink, and be merry, for tomorrow we die." It seems there is an urgency built in to the desire to fill our empty spaces, and that the time to begin is always in the present, and yet, many never seize the moment. When the desire for fulfillment crops up, the mind automatically becomes awakened and sets in motion the process of finding solutions. It is said that we human beings do not change unless there is a serious emotional episode taking place in our lives. When such an event occurs, the mind is quickened into action and the feature of the mind to search for options or to perceive alternatives steps to the forefront. This is exemplified in the episode dealing with the disciples, when Jesus was no longer their guide and Peter, recognizing they had nothing to eat said, "I am going fishing," and the other disciples who were with him said, "We are going too." Peter represents faith: the perceiving power of the mind able to link itself to or capture ideas and out of them have hope for new opportunities and possibilities.

Faith is a combination of mentally seeing and at the same time having hope. Faith helps to wipe out the shadows in the dance of human existence. "If you have as much faith as a grain of mustard seed you can say to the mountain, be removed."

Let's be blunt. If there is no image on your mental screen, how can you hope for it? Where there is no hope, despair reigns, and there is no chance of experiencing a new heaven. The combination of seeing and expecting are important in the manifesting business, of which we are all engaged twenty-four-seven.

When faith is active, it stirs the other spiritual qualities connected to the creative process, in which love and imagination are prominent. Love attracts other ideas associated with the one first caught in the net, while imagination shapes them. "We walk by faith, not by sight." Before we can successfully use faith in the development of a better life, we must become aware of our spiritual nature by understanding that the universal flow of substance is present at all times, in all places, and we are inlets and outlets of it.

There is no doubt that the mind is a marvelous utensil, with a vast array of qualities to tap into and use the substance in its midst. Through these qualities of mind we are able to observe, perceive, translate, interpret, express, expand and experience. These and many more are possible through the gift of imaging called thinking.

Thinking can be likened to the crafting of mental images from the nothingness, ideas of which all things are made. Ideas are like floating cells in the universe and our minds are like nets able to catch, decode and shape them based on individual standards. The mind is our workshop and laboratory in which we work each moment of the day, formulating and synthesizing ideas in accordance with the desires entertained. Thinking is man's true power, for through it he builds his life, affairs and world while adding value to them. Whatever we think about, we have the capability to manifest visible replicas.

The writer of Job introduces us to another factor in gaining our potential. He writes, in Chapter 22, Verse 28, "You will decide on a matter, and it will be established for you." One must be specific in one's decision-making. "One cannot serve two masters at the same time"; "A double-minded man is unstable in all his ways." To be specific, one must quickly come to a decision. Constant vacillating destroys the power of now, which feeds the engine of completion.

Before we go on, we should bear in mind that each of us began like all other aspects of the created universe: unformed substance, still in the process of becoming, always moving toward the invisible potential that is at the center of our being. In the same manner, within the egg lies the potential of a chicken, so within us lies the Christ ideal, which under the right conditions seeks to emerge. We are always journeying to the unknown, the hidden we cannot see with our human eye but through faith we get glimpses, and by hoping and affirming we draw it closer and closer. Somehow we are all aware that there is something to get beyond what we now have, hence the constant search for more. As Jesus said to his students, "Be perfect as your heavenly father is perfect." Perfection is a spiritual ideal no human being can ever attain, but must still seek.

One may see the preferred state and expect it to come forth, but there is no magic in the process. The poet says, "Nothing is gained without sweat and blood." This corresponds with a part of the creative allegory in the scene after man disobeyed the Creator and hid himself from its presence. God pronounced, "By the sweat of his brow that he would eat bread." The eating of bread denotes the creative process of ingestion, digestion, appropriating and assimilating, in other words: work. Man must be actively engaged in the process of turning his desires into manifestations. "Faith without works is dead."

The work required is mainly mental. Faith, Love and Imagination have produced the images that can lead to the state of contentment, but we must decide what images best represent our expectation. This is where Wisdom, Understanding and Order help us to analyze, quantify, rationalize, and have clarity to set the process in motion that can lead to fulfillment. This is the stage where strength is needed, that in us which produces the doggedness and courage to proceed, the perseverance that allows the hyena to fill itself after patiently pursuing its prey until victory is won.

Then Strength is linked with Enthusiasm. The strong sensations necessary to plant the seeds in the garden of the mind are developed, and in due season they will manifest after their kind. Desire turned into intent and coupled with feeling is the combination necessary for successful germination; the stronger the sentiment the greater the chance for development.
Will, the executive factor of the mind, sends out to Order and with Power declares, "All authority is given unto heaven and on earth," and existences begin through the Life forces in the subjective phase of mind.

Before we send the intent to the nursery, we need to call forth the eliminating quality to set aside all opposing forces; hence, somewhere in the process we must do a forgiveness treatment.

Forgiveness is a double-action procedure. It is the giving up of the old and the planting of the new. It is a change that takes place. If your hands are full, they must be emptied before they can hold anything else. As one writer termed it, "Go sell all that you have and then come and follow." Forgiveness is a constant activity, and one must consciously be engaged in it at all times. Without it we would be "putting new wine in old wineskins."

Sometimes in my classes, I get this question: How come no one ever told me I am a spiritual being with infinite potential, and that I am not bound by what appears to be? One of the answers I give is: when the student is ready, the student begins the search to know, with the intent to become.

Only when one is awakened to the truth of one's being can one do planned growth by using one's faculties in a scientific matter. Having removed the blinkers of ignorance, like Paul did during his conversion, when all the scales and the binding chains of archaic beliefs were lifted and he began the metamorphic process of being the great evangelist that he eventually became, the latent giant within was awakened. Immediately after awakening, in his semi-confused state, he withdrew to the desert, where the new seeds of hope could replace the old limiting ones, and where out of conflict, a new person was born. This is the same route Jesus took after his realization of his spirituality.

It is important to come to the same understanding as these two giants did: that we need to come apart to know what we hope is possible by refraining from activities that reinforce old attitudes and behaviors. In this state we come to experience the true nature of being, that we are each spiritual organisms, operating as cells in the collective body of God. As cells, we are all important to the well-being of the whole, that although we are unique and individualized, we each have a special function to play in the overall plan. As a cell operating in the body of God, God is in each of us and each one in God: hence, there is no separation, and each is commissioned to do the will of the whole. Jesus expressed this idea in these ways when he said, "I and the father are one"; "If you see me you have seen the father"; and, "Let the mind that was in Christ Jesus be in you."

Once the new program is in place, one must continuously believe in one's ability to produce the desired outcomes.

Some of the Challenges

Ignorance of the nature of being: We are always successfully bringing forth the fruits of our labors. Nothing can occur in our lives and experience without being a product of the mind. The laws of creation are exact—"What we sow, we reap"; "As we think in our hearts so are we." The emotion we attach to a thought gives it its nature; believing it is difficult makes it difficult, for that is the pronouncement. We must remember that the entire process from the beginning to the end is of our own creation, and that the only one experiencing it is its Creator, having made it all, declares it as good. Having been created after the divine pattern, we operate in accordance with its mode of operation.

Fear: Many people, not knowing their divine heritage, struggle in their pursuit of their dreams because of fear. They give power to the shadows cast from their beliefs in appearances. Fear has no power. It piggybacks on the power to perceive and hope for, but instead of receiving impulses from the spiritual universe, it comes to rely on those received via the five senses as interpreted by the subjective phase of mind.

In the discovery of self, divine potential, one realizes that nothing can constrain you, not even what you might have previously been afraid of. You can stand before Pilate and say, "I don't have to prove who I am before you."

Dragging One's Feet: It appears that most of us believe we will live forever and that time is stored in a warehouse and whenever we need some we can place an order, and as a result we forget the now factor. In reality we only have now; yesterday is a memory held in mind and tomorrow is always coming but never does. The habit of waiting for God or someone else to do the work is one of the seeds sown by a belief system that says this benevolent man or king who rewards us in accordance with our deeds will eventually bestow upon us that for which we beg. Many live at this terminal, waiting for the plane or ship to come in. "Seek and you shall find." Seeking requires action, and action does it.

Abram observed his father, whose intent was to prosper by going to Canaan but for some reason tarried in Haran and died there without attaining the full measure of his intent. Abram got up and went on his quest, which took him to many lands and many experiences out of which he prospered greatly.

There is the story of the ten lepers in 2 Kings 8, who lived outside the gates of Jerusalem. While they watched the people within its walls die of starvation, they decided one night to get up and go in search of food. As they approached the tents of the Assyrians, the soldiers thought they heard the sound of chariots and fled, leaving all their supplies behind. The lepers served themselves, and became the saviors of the inhabitants of Jerusalem. Desire is a calling that needs to be answered now.

Consider the phrase, "Time is the distance between two points of interest, it does not exist." There is a phenomenon of the mind that allows us to relate and link two mental images together, thereby creating movement. In reality there is no movement, it is the mind that creates it. This is borne out in motion pictures, where twenty-four frames of still images are shot within a second; the viewer plays this back and sees movement. This is possible because the mind does not forget. It is the same with time. We are presented with individual movement that we link in our mind to form the illusion of time. Procrastination comes from us believing we have time, when we only have now. This practice of not making a decision or putting it off can lead to regret, which can sink a soul into the dark hole of frustration, anger and jealousy. To see others fulfill their dreams as yours fall into empty fantasies is but to die.

Duality: The battle for control of the mind is an ongoing one, when the dominant forces of the old order seek to overwhelm the newly discovered truths one seeks to plant in mind. Emile Cady calls it chemicalization. This is expressed by the synoptic gospel writer in their handling of the change of thinking that occurred in Jesus, as described in the baptism narrative. As soon as Jesus realized his divinity, at the crossing point, the River Jordan, he journeyed to the wilderness: the state of mixed vegetation. This is where his old thought pattern, represented by the devil, began to seek to exert its opposition to his newfound inspiration. This is the stage when we question our ability based on past performance, and where emotions of fear, doubt, worry and frustration are brought into play, for the devil in us is vicious and cunning, playing on our emotions to kill the new.

Failure to Listen: The inability to surrender to spirit becomes a major stumbling block to growth, believing you know how to get to the unknown. What helps me is when I can remind myself I have never been to this moment before, therefore, I don't know what to do. In that moment of being conscious, I allow myself to become the servant of spirit, so it may lead me in the paths of right thinking. I often declare, "Of myself I can do nothing." In this act of surrender, I make myself available to the many ways that spirit has to solve any seeming problem.

Self-Proclamation: Another obstacle to growth is falling into the trap of believing one's own advertisement. In the temptations of Jesus, the devil—the usurping self—realizing that Jesus had experienced his oneness with the Divine, said to him on the pinnacle of the temple, "Throw yourself down," for it is written, 'He will give his angels charge of you.'" It is easy after attaining some measure of success to trumpet one's horn, to be seen of men as a miracle worker. To even set out to be recognized by others goes against the laws of spirit. It is the meek who inherit the earth, and the proud and hoity-toity are humbled.

Wasted Energy: The greatest squander is the waste of one's energy, for that is really all we have and what we are. When we engage in frivolous activities that do not lead us to fulfillment, this only saps our energy. Our wasted thoughts, words or deeds are not redeemable. It is sad to see someone arriving at the workstation of the mature, and have regrets for not having lived a dream. The pain can be great. Every living thing seeks to become a likeness of the prototype it carries. The egg, the seed, the sperm, are starting points of energy coded with information of a potentiality. Every conscious moment should be spent in activity that promotes fulfillment.

Opinions of Others: Waiting for, seeking after and relying on the advice of others is another challenge. There is an inner voice that, if we train ourselves to listen to it, is all we need to guide us in the paths we need to travel. Sometimes we should look and see that those we seek out for advice are sometimes more flawed and incompetent than we are.

Inflexibility: One of the most powerful stories given to us is found in Luke, and it's the story of the man with two sons. In it, Jesus portrays a soul that is seeking to find itself. It refers to a young man who sets out on a journey with the full blessings of his father. As he traveled far away from his comfort zone and the support of his father, he encounters many experiences that caused him to break with some of the traditions he had known. He had to support himself, and he became a servant of others. He had to mix and appropriate with what he was taught to be unclean. In other words, he had to be flexible in order to sustain life. It was because of this ability to adapt and change his mind that he came to his senses, and in that moment appreciated his father as the true source and supply in his life. The other brother, who stayed at home, never learned to appreciate what he had, for he was inflexible, seriously self righteous and selfish.

Being flexible is important to our growth. It is the willow that survives the big storms; the rigid oak falls. Those who believe their beliefs are universal truth become like Lot's wife, a crystallized state in which there can be no expansion.

Seeking Satisfaction from the Outside: All that comes from the outer are the likeness produced by our subconscious mind; if we are therefore not happy within, how can that which we form make us satisfied?

There is a desire built into all living things: the need to experience more. This is a spiritual quality at the heart of every man. Our need for improvement and the need to overcome are essential qualities in the drive that leads us forward.

Culture Boxes: When Abram was inspired to move to a new consciousness, he realized that to do so, he had to leave his father's house and his kin behind. These represent the tribal practices and religious concepts he had known. These old mental patterns act as filters that cause us to view the world and ourselves through myopic windows that never allow us to open the shades on the truth. Moving away from these old ways of living and seeing things is important if we need to grow, especially those who are religious.

Religious concepts are never carved in stone, and must be allowed to evolve. If not, they become albatrosses around our necks. All forms of fundamentalist thinking are dangerous and lead to stagnation. We must allow ourselves to have inlets and outlets. Each generation must expand on the concepts of the previous. It is man's mission and duty to "be fruitful and multiply," and "fill the earth and subdue it."

Notes

_____

_____

_____

_____

_____

_____

_____

_____

_____

_____

_____

About The Author

The Reverend Alice J. Brown is the senior minister of Living Truth Center for Better Living (LTC) in East Cleveland, Ohio where she leads and teaches her congregation through inspirational lessons and practical tips on how to follow the example of our wayshower, Jesus the Christ. Living Truth Center is an affiliate of the Universal Foundation for Better Living (UFBL), an independent new thought organization, founded by the legendary Reverend Dr. Johnnie Colemon, currently lead by the Reverend Dr. Mary A. Tumpkin, who serves as the President.

Reverend Alice's path to senior minister began more than thirty years ago when she was first introduced to the teachings at Christ Universal Temple (CUT) in Chicago, Illinois. She found the positive messages to be quite inspirational and very practical. She was able to apply the teachings in her own life with much success and knew she wanted to help others do the same. Reverend Alice started her UFBL journey with a teaching license where she still teaches classes through the Johnnie Colemon Theological Seminary (J.C.T.S.).She further studied to earn her counseling license and was ordained as a minister in October 1995.

Reverend Alice was appointed a staff minister at Christ Universal Temple by Reverend Colemon and served in numerous positions from board member of the UFBL where she served as secretary to becoming the JCI registrar, a UFBL Licensed Teacher/Counselor, member of the prayer ministry at CUT, to being a published author of the UFBL monthly publication the Daily Inspiration to working with the Writer's Guild.

Prior to her appointment as Living Truth Center's senior minister, Reverend Alice was the Founding Minister-Director of Universal Oneness for Better Living Satellite Center in Chicago Heights, IL, a satellite of Christ Universal Temple. She served as the Minister Director for 14 years where there were over 25 people who received their "Master's Certificate," and 7 who received their "Master Plus Certificates," and in 1997 she was awarded The Minister of the Year Award by the Eta Phi Beta sorority, Alpha Lambda Chapter.

Reverend Alice has spoken at various churches, women's groups, and other organizations to spread the message on how to live a better life by applying practical and spiritual lessons to everyday living experiences. She is a frequent contributing writer to Daily Inspiration for Better Living and has contributed to the JCI News Link, and the Grapevine Newsletter, a UFBL publication. She has also conducted numerous workshops, seminars, and empowerment clinics on topics such as forgiveness and healing. With her unique blend of personal stories and positive affirmations, she is helping others understand that there is a better way to live.

Not one to rest on her laurels, Reverend Alice continued to expand her knowledge; on May 10, 2008, she received her BA degree in Christian Ministry and Organizational Leadership from Trinity International University. She graduated Cum Laude. To honor Rev. Alice's continued commitment to academic excellence and scholarly leadership, her professors nominated her to Who's Who among Students in American Universities and Colleges.

Reverend Alice is most proud of her forty-six years marriage to Frank A. Brown, Sr. they are the parents of four children, grandparents of nine and the great-grandparents of one.

Rev. Alice J. Brown
Living Truth Center for Better Living, Inc.
1850 Belmore Road
East Cleveland, Ohio 44112
216.249.0330
www.livingtruthcenter.org
uoom@aol.com

- Seven -

Why We Must Leave Our Comfort Zone

By Rev. Alice J. Brown

Leaving our comfort zone allows us to not get stuck in the familiar. When we find ourselves moving through life without thinking and cannot remember moving through the day, week, month or year, we are leading mindless lives. Leaving a place of familiarity is not easy, especially when one might be leaving family, friends, and all else that has been a part of their life. Yet, when one is born, raised and transitioned in the same place, have they accomplished their divine plan? If we have a dream in our heart and we are afraid to follow the calling placed on our lives, we find ourselves among the walking dead. We are breathing, taking up space, but we are not feeling alive, or accomplishing the dream that has been placed in our hearts. Certainly, people can remain in the same location and not be in a comfort zone if they are heeding their call.

In *The Dream Giver*, Bruce Wilkinson states, "Like the genetic code that describes your unique passions and abilities, your Big Dream has been woven into your being from birth. You're the only person with a Dream quite like yours." The question is, are you living your dream, or are you stuck in a life of complacency? The main character in *The Dream Giver*, Ordinary, was willing to leave Familiar and follow his dream. He encountered many dangers, as well as met much joy on the way. Leaving Familiar was not easy; however, he made it, and is there encouraging each of us to follow him on the journey of a lifetime.

You might be asking the question, what is a comfort zone? You might also be saying that your life is content and you are happy as it is. That might be true to a degree. However, have you taken an inventory of your life lately and truly investigated your feelings about it? Are you really happy? Are you living the life you truly desire? Is there something you want to do, but are afraid to attempt because of your age, race, education, or some other perceived excuse? A comfort zone, according to Webster, is, "the temperature range within which one is comfortable. The level at which one functions with ease and familiarity." When we live this lifestyle we cannot grow, will not learn anything new or exciting, and are not challenged. In other words, we find ourselves declining or bored with ourselves as well as with our lives. When God has given you a dream and you choose not to give birth to it, you are cheating yourself as well as life in general. There is something only you can do in a unique and wonderful way. Each person came to earth with gifts and talents that will help people live healthy, happy, and prosperous lives.

What if you made your transition from the physical plane back into the spiritual, and you were asked when you arrived to empty your life bag and show all the things you accomplished during your time on earth? When you opened your bag, you found it empty because you had not done anything other than the daily, mundane things everyone does. What if you are asked to explain why you returned to the spiritual plane with so many undeveloped dreams? What if you are given an opportunity to look through a mirror and are shown the gifts you were supposed to leave behind, blessing those whose lives were touched with your talents? You then see all of those who were not blessed simply because you were too afraid to step out of your comfort zone and attempt to share what you came to earth to do. Now you are told that you must return to earth and not return to the spiritual zone until your life bag is rich with stories of how you dared to move beyond yourself and deliver what you came to earth to share.

There are many benefits for going beyond what you may think you can do. However, God uses ordinary people to do extraordinary things. We are all made in the image-likeness of God, and can have as far as we can see. How far can you see? The promises that God made with Abraham, Isaac, Moses, Jesus and others in the Bible are still true for us today.

We must live our lives with passion, determination and perseverance, and be willing to stretch ourselves in ways that might not be considered at the time.

What if Harriet Tubman-Ross had freed herself and left the others in slavery without attempting to guide those who were open and receptive to freedom? What if Abraham Lincoln had done what was easy and comfortable? Would African-Americans still be in slavery? We can look around and see many ordinary people who chose to go beyond what appeared to be a limitation and see how God brought them through. These people can serve as models for us, for they are pointing the way to live a life beyond just dreams and wishes.

We can even turn to the Bible for guidance, remembering Moses' mother, who was willing to sacrifice her son by putting him in the Nile River when Pharaoh had declared death on all Hebrew males up to two years of age.

Go back further to Abram, who left his country when God guided him to go to a foreign land, and he became the father of a nation. From his bravery, Jesus' lineage was established.

Move forward in the Bible and consider a very unlikely character, Paul, who helped establish churches in the name of Jesus after he dared to hunt, jail and slay those who were followers of Jesus. When you consider these examples, you can see how lives were improved for all of those who were touched by these people and their willingness to move out of their comfort zone.

Leaving your comfort zone is not easy. Yet it is rewarding once it is done. It is also humbling to look back in reflection as to how God was able to bring Abram, Paul, and Moses' mother out of their states of complacency. There are emotions that must be dealt with, such as fear, doubt, inferiority complex and other negative feelings that will come forth from the soul. God is always there taking care of us even when we aren't aware of it. Consider *Hinds' Feet on High Places* by Hannah Hurnard, whose character, Much Afraid, "traveled with Sorrow and Suffering." Much Afraid left her home in the valley of fear to follow the Shepherd as she traveled toward becoming a new creation in Christ Jesus. During her travels she was haunted by her family of negativity, who were determined not to allow her to leave fear behind. This is a wonderful reminder of all of the negativity within our souls. Yet we can leave our "family of negativity" behind by keeping our eyes on God, even when we are afraid, or there is fear, sorrow, suffering, sadness, and all other forms of negativity around us and within us.

There is a wonderful example of a woman who was willing to retire from her job, leave her family and start on a venture that led her to founding two ministries in two different cities and her helping a number of other ministries. Remember, she retired from a job she had worked for over twenty or so years and moved to a location where she knew no one, to assist a group of twelve people begin a ministry under Universal Foundation for Better Living, Inc. (better known as UFBL). This fantastic woman is the Reverend Ann H. Jefferson. She moved to Cleveland and assisted a study group that evolved into a UFBL Center in a very short period of time. This group of twelve grew rapidly. In two years, they were able to purchase a building of their own. That ministry, known as Living Truth Center for Better Living, Inc. is currently celebrating twenty-three years of doing God's business in the world. After seven years of ministering in Cleveland, she moved to Baltimore and assisted another ministry for the organization, with another group of people she did not know. They also moved from a Study Group to a Center and that ministry, known as One God One Thought, is still thriving. But, the Reverend Ann was not finished. She left Baltimore and moved to Las Vegas, and served the organization as the Eastern District Director. She worked with various Study Groups and Centers within her district, helping the leaders with her knowledge.

This woman left her comfort zone and ventured into the unknown, shaking in her boots, yet she touched and changed many lives for the better. This woman has made her transition. However, she proved what God can and will do when you are willing to step out on faith and allow God to use your life to benefit others. She not only built ministries, she mentored other leaders spiritually, and has left her mark on the lives of those she touched profoundly.

When there is a calling on your life, you must be willing to go when and where God calls. God did not send just those in the Bible, God is sending us today to go and minister to the world in a variety of ways. "God is Spirit" (John 4:24). But God works in each and every one of Its creations, and each of us were created by God. It is up to us to get up and go about the business of living lives that represent God in every way.

Of course there are times when life is difficult; people can overcome difficulty. A diamond begins as a dark piece of coal, but when it goes through the refining process and is put under heat and pressure, it turns into a beautiful gem desired by all. Follow the examples of the character who was willing to leave Familiar, and Much Afraid, who left the valley of fear and traveled with Sorrow and Sadness. God was always available when needed. On their journey they met faith, joy, peace, love, power, substance, life, wisdom, and many other soul qualities that sustained them while they ventured farther from what they knew and were comforted by. They found that lurking in the shadows were negative feelings, waiting to carry them back from where they had traveled. However, they were willing to let God fight their battles, surrendered all to God, and moved forward even when they did not understand why they were encountering so much opposition. They gained strength, understanding, patience, tolerance, and so many more qualities, and ended up stronger and wiser. Best of all, they had a closer relationship with God. They came to trust that God's Presence resided within them. And, when doubt and frustration showed up, as it will, they were willing to release these things to God and allow God to guide them through the storm of negativity.

Most people are forced to leave their comfortable lives when there is an explosion or eruption of some kind, even if they just move in their minds rather than in the physical realm. When all is settled and done, newness appears that was not seen before. Growth has taken place that would not have occurred otherwise. Bless the situations and circumstances, even if they are painful. Call them good and very good, and that is what they will become. When situations or circumstances show up that bring difficulty, get closer to God. Recall how Jesus never turned away from God, no matter how difficult the issue became. When his friend Judas, who walked with him and carried the purse, kissed him so he could be taken into custody, and Peter denied him and he was beaten and crucified, his faith never wavered. When those in his hometown of Nazareth attempted to throw him off the cliff, he moved away from them but not from God. Can we do the same? Yes, we can. We too can do the things Jesus did, and greater things than He did. How? By trusting God, taking everything to God in prayer, and doing what we are guided to do once we hear and understand the instructions. We do not know what wonderful plan God has in store for us. If we are not willing to take a risk, we might never find out what it is or what talents we have that the world might be given.

There are things we can do that cannot be done by another. "Be willing to be bad enough until you can get better." There is a musician who invited his family and friends over to hear him play the cello before he had perfected his craft. At first, all they heard was noise, and were irritated that he had the nerve to invite them to concerts before he could play the instrument. However, once he became a gifted artist, those who had endured the terrible sounds realized he had to make the clatter while learning to become the musician he eventually became.

There is a wonderful faculty located "between the eyes" of each of us, and is known as Imagination, "the Scissors of the Mind." This is the way people can begin to see themselves in their minds and move out of the old spaces to see them living the lives that are knocking at the door of their hearts, asking to be let out. Moving from the place of Familiar is not easy, but can be done in stages and steps. Begin to mentally see yourself doing what you want. Hold onto the dream until it becomes a reality.

Working with this faculty can be done by creating a "treasure map" or "vision board." This can be done by taking construction paper or a poster board and putting pictures on it of what you want and something that symbolizes God. Then, look at it several times a day to hold the image in your mind, seeing yourself as you desire until it comes forth. This sounds simple, yet it works. It works because of the way our minds are built. "As we think in our hearts so are we" (Proverbs 23:7 KJV paraphrase). In other words, what we think about we bring about. This is the law of thinking.

There is an example of a person who had a dream of receiving a college degree. This person married and started a family without her high school diploma. Yet she always knew that one day she would earn a college degree. She went back to school and received her high school diploma while working and raising her family. She and her husband took turns attending school so one of them would be with the children at night. After the last child had completed his college degree, she saw this as her opportunity to return to school. Over the years, the person attended various classes and became accomplished at several trades, but it was important to her to receive her college degree. At the right time, she returned to college, and four years later received her college degree and was listed in Who's Who Among Students in American Universities and Colleges. She also graduated cum laude. How was this possible? One reason is that this person believed that it was going to happen; she never gave up on her dream. She treasure mapped for the degree, and she was willing to do the work necessary to obtain her goal. She was willing to move out of her comfort zone and did not allow her age or anything else to discourage her. She is now a role model for her children, grandchildren, and others in her family as well as her friends. Accomplishing her aspiration lifted her self-esteem greatly, so much so, she encourages others to return to school and not allow the past to be a deterrent.

Continue to mentally see yourself as you desire until it becomes your reality. This cannot be stated enough. Look at those around us who stood up for their beliefs and made a difference for those around them. If Nelson Mandela had gone along with the status quo, South Africa would not be free today. If Dr. Martin Luther King had not been willing to organize and march, would African Americans be able to vote, or live and work where they choose? Would we have the first African American President? There are others in our family, our friends, and local citizens who we can use as an example of those moving out of their comfort zone and doing what they are being called to do.

If you are a person who has learned a lot during your time of living, you can also help those around you by teaching others what you know. This is another way of moving out of your comfort zone. Think about those young ones around you who have not yet learned how to live life successfully; they are looking for someone to mentor them. Create a flyer of your talents, skills and gifts, and offer to share them with those who are interested in learning them, or create a booklet of your talents, skills and gifts, sharing it in written form. There is a wonderful cook who created recipes, and had people willing to pay her to prepare special dishes for them. This person was given not one, but two tape recorders, and asked to speak the recipes into it so it could be transcribed into a cookbook. The person made her transition without recording or writing down her recipes, and so did the great dishes she created. This is a prime reason to leave our comfort zone. If you choose not to, you will return to the Spiritual realm with an empty bag, thus depriving the world of your special talents, skills and gifts. Leaving one's comfort zone is not always easy, yet it can be done. Think of the reward that comes along with being willing to step outside your well-known world and walk into one not known by you. Consider the females who decided to go into the military. In today's society, the women go to war with the men and they fight side-by-side, which is not how it has always been. They are leaving family and friends behind instead of it always being the other way around. Returning home can be challenging when they have been out of the mode of being the homemaker. There are several young women who decided they were not ready for college, therefore they joined the military. Their parents talked to them about what they had to expect. They chose to join anyway, and were with the first group shipped out when the war in Iraq started. These young women returned home safe; however, they truly were not comfortable. We don't recommend you take this route, yet you can live your dream, whatever it may be. These young women are now out of service and attending college. They are very serious about their education, and it is a joy knowing they stepped out of their comfort zone, even when they were not sure of the outcome.

You too can leave your comfort zone, by being willing to live the life that might now merely be a dream. Take one step at a time while moving forward, trusting that it will become a reality in due season, knowing God is there to guide you on the path by "making the rough roads smooth, and the crooked ones straight." Therefore, be willing to feel the fear or other negative feelings that might show up, yet persevere. Do not give up. Pray, meditate, and spend time in the silence with God, getting the strength, courage and fortitude that will sustain you on your journey away from commonplace.

The reason we must leave our comfort zone is so we can share the talents and skills we were born with, so we can be a blessing as well as give a blessing. Our willingness to move outside our comfort zone can bring blessings to people we might never meet. And there will be a level of satisfaction that cannot be explained. Just as the minister who founded two ministries and worked with a variety of others has blessed those she ministered to as well as others she never met. Think of it this way: "Of myself I do nothing, it is the Father within me that does the work." Within each of us dwells the Christ, which is the individualization of God, which is guiding us toward our soul's desire. There is a prayer we can pray that will provide us hope as we strive to live the lives we were born to live:

> The Presence of God goes before me to make the rough places smooth and the crooked places straight; that same Presence remains behind me as a blessing and benediction to all who pass my way. It also walks beside me leading, guiding and directing me.

Resources

http://www.prayerfoundation.org/books/book_review_hinds_feet_on_high_places.htm

Wilkinson, Bruce. The Dream Giver. Colorado Springs: Multnomah Books, 2003

Holy Bible (KJV & NRSV)

Notes

_____

_____

_____

_____

_____

_____

_____

_____

_____

_____

ABOUT THE AUTHOR

Robert Henderson Jr. CFP

Robert Henderson is the President and CEO of the Henderson Financial Group, a Financial Planning and Investment Company with offices in Miami Florida and Charlotte North Carolina. He has conducted seminars and workshops all over the United States, Canada, South America and the Caribbean islands. An expert in financial Planning and investment strategies, Mr. Henderson is a Certified Financial Planner (over 25 years) and holds securities licenses in stocks, bonds, and mutual funds. He is also a licensed independent insurance broker as well as a licensed real estate broker. Founded in 1992 by Robert Henderson Jr. The Henderson Financial group is committed to educating and serving people from all over the world who aspire a more spiritual and prosperous life. His goal is to demystify the world of investment and money management to those who ask, seek, and knock. His motto is "we don't teach with words, we teach with meaning, we explain finances to you as though we were talking to a 6yr old, plain and simple".

Mr. Henderson is an author, radio host (Miami Fl and Charlotte NC) and new paper columnist, he has written hundreds of published articles on all aspects of financial planning. He's a motivational speaker and weekly blogger on his website newundergroundrailroad.com. He volunteers as a guardian Ad-Litem and the voice for homeless and disadvantage children. Mr. Henderson strongly believes that the fruits that we bare are as the result of our thoughts and what we think about. He is a member of the Universal Truth Center for better living located in Miami Florida. He sees the outer world and all its happenings as projections of the inner world of imagination. "There's no limit to your imagination therefore, there's no limit to you".

Contact:

The Henderson Financial Group

5783A NW 151 Street

Miami Lakes, Fl 33014

(305) 825-1444

Finance1444@bellsouth.net

www.roberthendersonjr.com

- Eight -
Your Right to Be Rich

By Robert Henderson Jr. CFP ®

It is your right to be rich. Yes, that's right, your right. You don't have to beg, borrow or steal; you and I were created by the source of everything that is. We are all here to lead an abundant life filled with peace, love and happiness. We are here to demonstrate and illuminate the unlimited power and grace of our Creator. None of us should be living from paycheck to paycheck, broke, busted and disgusted. We have been created in the image of our Creator, and since we are of the same image, we must therefore create. When we don't create we sin, and the word "sin" means to miss the mark. We were born with a special key; this key is the key to life. It's the key that unlocks unlimited wisdom, and our right to be rich is buried deep within our consciousness. To have this key and use this key is our birthright. All we have to do is ask, seek, and knock. In other words, believe, have faith, and work toward a worthy goal, and the door shall be open to you. This is not only a promise, it's the law. The Almighty has already given us everything we want and need. All we have to do is open our eyes—no, not our mortal eyes, for our mortal eyes have caused us not to see. Our mortal eyes judge by appearance and are slave to our senses. We must begin to see with our spiritual eyes, for when we learn to see with our spiritual eyes we begin to see the truth. And the truth shall set you free. You can only find this truth by studying your deep self. And as you dig deep, you will find the treasures of heaven inside your conscious and subconscious mind. It is where moth and rust do not consume, and where thieves do not break through and steal (Matt 6:20). Knowledge of the law of consciousness, and understanding the method of operating this law, will enable you to accomplish all you desire in life. And when you accomplish all you desire in life, brothers and sisters, you are rich.

Notes

_____

_____

_____

_____

_____

_____

_____

_____

_____

_____

About The Author

Rev. Dr. Anna Price, Ph.D.

After 25 years as an administrator (Director of Upward Bound and Assistant Athletic Director for Student Services, Assistant Provost), **Dr. Anna Price, Ph.D.** retired from the University of Miami in 1997. Ordained in that same year, Dr. Price began serving as Executive Pastor at the Universal Truth Center for Better Living. In July 2008, Dr. Price also completed an 18 month tenure as a Prison Chaplain with the Florida Department of Corrections. Her community involvements have included: Chairperson of the Historical Museum of South Florida, Vice Chair of the Dade County Commission on the Status of Women, President of the Coral Gables Democratic Women's Club, Member of the Florida Sports Foundation, and Recording for the Blind and Dyslexic. She was elected Mayor in the City of South Miami in 1997 (serving 9 months), where she had also served as Commissioner for 15 months. Dr. Price currently serves as Executive Minister and Outreach Minister at the Universal Truth Center as well as Provost/Academic Dean of the Johnnie Colemon Theological Seminary. She is a proud member of Delta Sigma Theta Incorporated.

Rev. Dr. Anna M. Price

Universal Truth Center for Better Living

21310 N.W. 37th Avenue

Miami Gardens, Florida 33056

305.624.4991

www.utruthcenter.org

aprice55@aol.com

- Nine -
Reshaping Your Character

By Rev. Dr. Anna Price, Ph.D.

The real object of life is not making money or becoming famous but the building of character, the bringing forth of the potentialities that exist in every one of us.

Jesus taught bigness of character to his followers.
— *Prosperity,* Charles Fillmore p. 161

The character of an individual is made up of the mental and moral qualities distinctive to that individual. It is the character of a person that determines the thoughts, feelings, words, actions, and reactions that dominate that person's life. It is the character of a person that determines how a person interacts with his environment and other people.

People whose characters are respectful of others, strive to be productive members of society, and follow the laws of the land

are considered to be those with strong characters. Others, who are disrespectful of others and their property and use unlawful means to promote and/or provide for themselves, are called criminals and are incarcerated: placed in correctional institutions (jails, prisons) where their characters can be reshaped or be permanently removed from society. The number of people in these places and the degree to which they do not recommit crimes and become productive members of society is a measure that can be used to determine the success of these reshaping efforts.

According to a 2008 report by the Pew Center, "The United States incarcerates more people than any country in the world, including the far more populous nation of China." This same report states that 2,319,258 are in prison or jail: 1,596,127 in state and federal prison custody and 723,131 in local jails. It concludes that this is a result of a steady expansion that has characterized the U.S. penal system for more than fifty years.

The philosophy that supports a system of incarcerating people who violate laws is threefold. First, it is designed to protect the broader community. Second, it punishes the violators. Third, it is designed to rehabilitate people: reshape their characters enabling them to live in harmony with others. The first two purposes are fulfilled by the very nature of incarceration. The third purpose is to transform—change form—or reshape the character of those who have violated the civil laws of the land. Historically, transformation of character, changing behavior, is associated

119

with a religious conversion—even in prison. The separation of violators of the law from others ultimately has as its purpose to prepare them to function in society without repeating these violations.

The process of reshaping/transforming character as reflected in the history of prisons parallels the spiritual unfolding of humankind as presented in Bible stories when interpreted metaphysically. Most specifically the liberation of children of Israel by Moses from slavery in Egypt as described in the Hebrew Bible and the Easter story as described in the New Testament.

Religion & Prisons

In his 1777 report titled "The State of the Prisons in England and Wales, with preliminary observations, and an account of some prisons" (as cited in Craig 1994), John Howard described the conditions of prisons during his time as places where prisoners: lacked water, air, and sewage disposal; were tortured; and were crowded with wives and children of debtors. Howard did not consider these conditions conducive to his view of the purpose of the penitentiary: Described by Craig as a "man of deep Christian piety," Howard viewed the penitentiary as an institution to separate prisoners from society in order that they have an opportunity to reflect on what they had done, repent, and be reformed.

Included in his recommendations to the magistrates of the British Parliament was that they select a chaplain to be assigned to each jail. Specifically regarding the chaplain, Howard recommended that the chaplain be a Christian who would counsel the prisoners as well as officiate services. In other words, these places, as they existed, were not conducive to transformation.

> In colonial America, biblical precepts provided the justification for punishment and, at times, a guideline for its severity. Hence, in Massachusetts, the maximum number of whippings was set at forty, as indicated by Old Testament scripture. Religion's influence in punishment remained apparent in the 19th century with   the development of the penitentiary.
> — Ignatieff, 1978, McKelvey, 1977

> Time spent in labor and reflection was to equip the offender with a spiritual coat or armor, capable of deflecting the most virulent of moral diseases
> — Clear p. 54

Influenced by the Howard report, religious groups in the United States became a part of the evolution of prisons in the United States from that characterized above to more humane institutions. Most notable among these groups were the Quakers (Craig, p. 55). The first institution in the United States that would fit the category of a "Correctional Institution" was the Walnut

Street Jail in Philadelphia, Pennsylvania, established by the Quakers in 1787 (Church of Christ Prison Ministry). A preacher named William Rogers began teaching the Bible there in that year. This component of the prison was believed the best way to correct the inmates of their erring ways. Prisons in the United States are a part of what is called the "correctional system."

Teaching values and morals based on the Bible, and the need for behavior to be consistent with them, are based on the belief that such behavior will be rewarded by a life in heaven after death. Continuing to violate these values and morals will result in going to hell after death. God is taught as a punishing and rewarding entity that controls the world and answers prayers for those who follow His instructions written in the Bible. In this model, people are taught that when they are tempted to violate God's laws, they are to pray to God to change them.

A New Model

Until the discoveries of Copernicus and Galileo, the church was trusted as the source to explain the mysteries of life. As science has progressed and provided logical/testable explanations for phenomena of the universe, many people are looking for explanations that do not solely depend on "faith." Today, scientists tell us "that the mind is the creative cause of all that transpires in the life of man, that the personal conditions are the results of man's action, that all the actions of man are the direct outcome of his ideas, that we never make a move of any kind until we first form

122

some image or plan in the mind" (Working With the Law, p. 14). Scientists have determined that the universe is governed by laws.

The teaching of New Thought Christianity is based on the teaching of Jesus and the belief that the true nature of humankind is spiritual, and that when it recognizes and accepts this truth, humankind will be empowered to understand that it is one with God and does not need an intermediary to hear the direction of God and can live the life God intended as taught by Jesus: "Do not be afraid, little flock, for it is your Father's good pleasure to give you the kingdom" (Luke 12:32 NRSV).

Reshaping character requires a change in attitude, mental position as to one's self-identity. The association of religion and prisons reflects the understanding that reshaping character requires acceptance of a religious teaching, and/or having a religious experience.

All people who strive to reshape their characters are not in a literal prison. However, they are in the prison of carnality, a belief that they are only human. The way to reshape character and free themselves is to become aware of who they are, connect with the source (God) through meditation, learn the laws of the universe and practice those laws.

When we understand that Universal Law is always expressing itself through intuition and how it operates in nature, we have heard the voice of the Lord.

The recognition and acceptance of our spiritual identity empowers us to study the Laws of Mind. The reshaping of character requires a movement in mind that changes our belief system.

The association of the mind and life experiences of humankind are expressed in the Holy Scriptures: "As a man thinketh in his heart so is he" (Proverbs 23:7); "Do not be conformed to this world, but be transformed by the renewing of your minds, so that you may discern what is the will of God—what is good and acceptable and perfect" (Romans 12:2).

The ruling state of mind reflects one's belief system— understanding that belief is "an inner acceptance of an idea as true" (The Revealing Word). Jesus taught that our life experiences are a reflection of what we believe: "Let it be done according to your belief...." (Matthew 8:13 KJV).

Reshaping your character requires a change in what you believe. The ruling state of mind is made up of various mental attitudes, which the individual adopts toward things, events, and life in general. If his attitudes are broad in mind, optimistic in tone, and true to life, his predominant mental state will correspond and exhibit a highly constructive and progressive tendency (Working With the Law, p. 27).

When we believe that outer conditions determine our experiences and that we are separate from our good/God, we live our lives as if controlled by outer conditions and circumstances. The reshaping of character from carnal to spiritual leads to a life of happiness, joy, peace and love. Spiritual character is the true estimate of the qualities of humankind. Building character from sense to spiritual "is ever from within outward." "Spiritual discernment of the reality of the origin of humankind's origin and being in God is the only enduring foundation of character." This happens in the silence.

Practical Application

The universe operates through laws that are designed to sustain itself. Even those events that we label as disasters—earthquakes, hurricanes, tornadoes—actually occur when there is a condition of imbalance. The universe is always seeking balance—homeostasis; the human body also operates on this principle. The New Thought Movement is one based on the mind science that was expressed in the Bible in Romans 12:2: "Do not be conformed to this world, but be transformed by the renewing of your minds, so that you may discern what is the will of God"—what is good and acceptable and perfect. One of the organizations that identifies itself with that movement is the Universal Foundation for Better Living. Its first statement, describing what it believes, states: "We believe it is God's will that every individual on the face of this earth should live a healthy, happy and prosperous life."

If any person is experiencing anything other than health, happiness and prosperity, there must be a transformation of the mind. This transformation can occur by reshaping the belief system by meditating regularly with the objective to:

- Accept that it is God's pleasure to give us the kingdom.

- Accept that God is no respecter of persons.
- Accept the power of the mind.
- Accept that as within, so without.
- Accept that we attract to ourselves what we are.
- Accept that we can reshape our character.
- Deny any belief that there is more than God.
- Replace those beliefs with attributes of God: love, life, peace, joy, and prosperity.
- Watch God work!

Notes

_____

_____

_____

_____

_____

_____

_____

_____

_____

_____

About The Author

The Reverend Derrick Wells is on a mission. That mission involves encouraging humanity to awaken to the sacred self and to live a life rooted in love. Rev. Wells embarked on a quest of personal development and transformation. He was capti- vated by the philosophy of Christian Metaphysics and was ordained as a U.F.B.L. minister by New Thought pioneer, the Reverend Dr. Johnnie Colemon.

Reverend Wells has served as an instructor in the Johnnie Colemon Institute; as Vice President of the Christ Universal Temple Board of Directors; and as a member of the U.F.B.L. Teaching Core. Derrick is an inspirational and spiritually gifted speaker. He is noted for his ability to speak to both the heads and hearts of his listeners. As a national and international presenter, he is known to be one of the foremost leaders, teachers and speakers in the Metaphysical and Better Living movement in America. He is also well known for the depth, insight, enthusiasm, and information he brings to his presentations.

A Critical Scholar, this Chicago native is a member of Lambda Pi Eta Honors Society and the National Communica- tion Association. His lectures, workshops, seminars, and training sessions cover a range of topics, among those are: spirituality, transformational leadership, personal empowerment, and orga- nizational psychology.

"A life lived in love is a life lived indeed," says Wells. It's a motto he lives by and seeks to spread through his speaking, writing, and living.

Rev. Derrick B. Wells

Christ Universal Temple

11901 S. Ashland Avenue

Chicago, IL 60643

773.568.2282 www.cutemple.org revwells@cutemple.org

Ten

The Benefits of Change

By Rev. Derrick Wells

How is it possible that something we are used to experiencing moment by moment can sometimes create within us a compelling sense of discomfort, intimidation, or resistance? Unwittingly, for many of us such is the power of change. The Greek philosopher Plato expanded on Heraclites' notion when he offered, "Everything changes and nothing remains the same." Every person on the face of the earth experiences change. Some changes are more profound or drastic than others, but change occurs for each of us nonetheless. Even if we partake in like activities, our yesterday is not our today and our today will not be our tomorrow, again, all due to the properties of change.

As you read these words, your physiology is going through a multitude of changes. These changes are the links that enable you to process this particular stimulus in ways that are useful. As your eyes scan this page, light rays passing through your pupils are being changed into information your brain can constructively interpret. While your mind considers these words, it shifts between multiple associations. While your ears experience the resonance of your thoughts as you peruse and recite these words, it changes your cognitive schemas. And depending upon whether you accept or reject these same words, your mental maps become irrevocably altered, thus you are further drawn into the gravity-esqe pull of change.

However, your changes do not end there. While those changes are occurring, you are also going through other changes as you either settle in to this read or mentally scurry about with some of your attention distributed on this page, or on your environment, or perhaps on the things you need to do over the course of this day. Your breathing might be changing from long and deep to rapid and truncated breaths as you make the mental note that it is almost time to turn the page. Changes are constantly occurring within and around you. Some are benign and others are not. Some you are directing and others you cannot, for again, such is the nature of change.

Change is ubiquitous. Seconds change into minutes. Minutes change into hours. Hours change into days. Days to months, months to years, and years under the compulsion of change become lifetimes. As my minister and mentor Johnnie Colemon would often exclaim, "Change, we must!" And not even the most fervent defense can withstand the winds of change. And that's a good thing! Here I have just described only a modicum of the changes you might have gone through in the relatively short period of time it took you to read to this point.

No one can dispute that change is an inevitable part of life. But what is it that makes some change mindlessly easy and other change unbearably difficult? Should we choose to acknowledge the many clues provided us, we might more readily surrender the animus that makes "some change" difficult in exchange for the greater dimensions that await us. Change is the beginning of a new opportunity.

According to Dr. Michele McMaster, "We are usually not prepared for change when it happens." This sense of unpreparedness might be a catalyst for the proverbial knots that bind our creativity and limit our ability to experience the life-giving opportunities of change. Therefore, the remedy to experiencing the benefits of change might be found through the shift that takes place when preparation and a proper understanding of self meet opportunity. Emergence is the companion of change, and we are here faced with the promise, prospect, and growth that knowledge and change provides.

Though seldom used in recent history, the term "metanoia" is perfectly suited to illustrate how transformation or change happens to an individual. When we begin to discuss the aspects of preparing for and directing change, it must be noted that an intentional shift of mind is required if we are to move beyond the perception of there being a randomness by which one becomes the subject of undesired change. It must also be noted that a mental shift is required to direct one's personal power toward the specific aims through which the benefits of change are realized. Which leads us back to metanoia.

Metanoia is a change, shift, or transcendence ("meta" meaning "above" or "beyond," as in "metaphysics") of mind ("noia"—mind). It is an evolution in learning that produces the emergence of some quality, faculty, and/or aptitude that was not expressed before. Plainly stated, metanoia is the visible manifestation of the benefits of change. The Apostle Paul urged that we "be transformed by the renewing of the mind." A logical subtext of this perspective tells us that the thinking of the existing mind produced the present results in our life. A transformation and renewal of the mind must then open the way for us to experience the possibilities and potentialities of something different or good (read "better"). But how are we to know when this "manifestation" becomes manifest? How do we to know when change happens? When change occurs, we move from translation to transformation. Opportunity and progress are the beneficial by-products of change. As previously stated, a skill or ability surfaces whereby we are able to create something where heretofore we could not. Knowledge, freedom, growth, connectivity and intention are all beneficial innovations of this change. Change enables us to apply that which we have learned. And since this book is about prosperous living, it can rightfully be stated that a change in the quality of life we live, a shift in how we use our faculties to attract our good, and a transcendence of living beyond our existing level, represent the kind of benefits we deservedly seek while we apply a propensity for change.

Practically speaking, the concept of change implies a departure from one thing to another. While we prepare to move toward a more prosperous way of living and being, what is it we might be departing from, and what are we going to? While the answer might appear obvious, it is likely far less obvious than we think. When we consider the least-desirable things in our life, we can easily conclude those are the things we must change. But does changing the "thing" rid us of that innate magnetic appeal that drew the "thing" to us from the outset? Given that each of us is a generative force, the answer for most of us is decidedly "no." Unfortunately, when exploring the opportunity to receive the maximum benefits of change, it is not enough to simply change the outer effect, which was brought about by an inner cause or mental equivalent. The "mental equivalent," as Emmet Fox phrased it, is one of the attractors that release our creative power. These attractors draw to us experiences consistent with the nature of the attractor. Like begets like, thus we find ourselves going through situations, conditions, and circumstances we have either intentionally or unintentionally attracted. The implications of this are actually quite astounding for us, since it suggests that: (1) There really are no arbitrary occurrences and there is a synchronicity to that which we encounter, and (2) Everything you want to change, you can change. But you must first make the change at the appropriate level. For instance, if you find that you do not have the financial cache required to live the quality of life you desire to live (this might be one of the considerations you hold for prosperity), you must change your mental equivalent, for your mental equivalent serves as the pattern or model that precedes your actual experience. The lack of money substance might therefore be interpreted as a mental equivalent for lack. A proper change of this mental equivalent or mental model will provide you with the ability to attract and produce new results, thus opening the way for you to experience the benefits of change. If you want to experience the benefits of change, you must change your maps of cause and effect.

Some influence theorists suggest that two requirements are necessary to experience enduring change. These requirements are that the changes be of value to you, and that you be able to do whatever is necessary to bring about change. That's it. Though these requirements might exact a matter of personal delineation, they are not complicated propositions. The first necessitates self-awareness, which if you are reading this book, you have likely already encountered to some extent. For some it might require a little soul searching. For others, the answer might be right in front of you, i.e., a manifestation you no longer desire.

The value you place on directing your change can also be uncovered by asking yourself the following question: "What do I want to experience?" It's a simple question that, when approached from the standpoint of wholeness, can lead you straight to the core of your being, as well as to that which you value in change. To be clear, you might accept the recommendation from another with respect to what your value "should" be, but ultimately, you must truly determine the value for you.

But please take care to not confuse this question with others, such as, "What has my experience been?" Or, "Why don't things work out for me?" Or, "What have I become conditioned to experiencing?" Or, "What do others expect from me, or for me?" Or any of the other mind-numbing hurdles we find along the pathway. Questioning centered on what you actually want to experience reveals with specificity that which is of value and importance to you. It also helps eliminate peripheral aims you might have unknowingly adopted from some external persuasions. Through the second requirement for change, we gain a firsthand experience of something discussed earlier—the emergence of a once dormant capacity, skill, or quality, which adeptly suits and prepares us for change. Boldly affirm, "I have what it takes to bring about change!" Not convinced? Well, you should be! Because all it takes is [first] a change of mind. History is replete with individuals who learned they had what it took and could do what was necessary to bring about change. You might have voted for Barack Obama to be president, captivated by his message of change. That vote represents the emergence of a capacity many assumed they would never see in a lifetime. But again, change is everywhere, and it is accompanied by certain properties that enable us to explore new paradigms and process life in new and meaningful ways.

Abolitionist Harriet Beecher Stowe, who was consumed with rearing six children while writing on occasion, published Uncle Tom's Cabin, a novel of such potency, it is generally regarded as one of the causes of the Civil War. Sir Roger Bannister also comes to mind. Who was he? He was an individual who outpaced his mental equivalent. He ran roughshod over his own mental model, as well as over the mental models of those who preceded him, by being the first person to run a sub-four-minute mile. Christine Brown was in her eighties when she scaled the Great Wall of China. The list goes on and on.

Their grand accomplishments aside, think not that any one of these individuals possesses "something" more than you. You have the requisite talent, ability, and wherewithal needed to bring about change. What's more, you have the mind power to access the nether regions of creation and change. The question is, will you? You have what it takes to experience the benefits of change. You can live a prosperous life now. Abundance is within your reach. What's standing in your way?

Change the Terrible Two & Experience More

There are two prevalent mental models that limit the extent to which we lead prosperous lives. Naturally, this short list is not meant to serve as any sort of treatise on limitation. Just as each of us enjoys a distinguished fingerprint or DNA, we also each employ our own unique set of attractors to furnish our individual experience. Suffice it to say, each of us establishes a consciousness that serves as a strange attractor for an even stranger experience: an invocation of limitation.

Yet however strange, the common consent of limitation is easily found when we examine the fact that some thirty-seven-million Americans live below the poverty line. And millions more are said to struggle as they hover at or near that line. While thirty-seven-million-plus people might not represent the critical mass, it's certainly a large enough sample to warrant concern.

As Mark Victor Hansen famously said, "The best way to help the poor is to not be one." Rethinking "the terrible two" will enable us to undergo a mental transformation. It will open us to the opportunity and progress that lay in wait at the dawn of change. It will facilitate the emergence and realization of abilities you knew not of. Rethinking these will open your mind and infuse your heart to the innovation and creativity of your soul. It's time to walk through the door. On the other side, your prosperity awaits.

The first of the terrible two is the thought that a life full of prosperity is undeserved. Many factors can lead to the acceptance of this notion, though it is far from the truth. In fact, most every natural system is impelled toward some form of prosperity. The integration and diversity witnessed within an ecosystem provides prosperity to the environment at large. Love and humanity evolves from the prosperous union of two individuals. Businesses provide their patrons with services that enable those individuals to experience a form of prosperity. Patrons provide businesses with cash in exchange for services that allow businesses to experience prosperity.

Given that life evolves through progress and growth, prosperity is a natural inclination of livingness. Hence, in truth, the only things undeserving about a life full of prosperity are the thoughts and feelings we might hold in connection to the same. Charles Fillmore offered, "Prosperity is not wholly a matter of capital or environment but a condition brought about by certain ideas that have been allowed to rule in the consciousness." The outgrowth of a rich consciousness serves as the determining factor as to whether prosperity is deserved. It is not a matter of deed; it is a matter of consciousness. You deserve all you have the awareness to receive. Remember, it is not what you are without that holds back your prosperity. It is what you think you deserve; it is what you expect. Your expectation is your proclamation to the Universal Good. You were brought forth from the best for the best to be the best. To go without is the just rewards of those who choose to do so. You cannot be found undeserving, unless your thinking dictates otherwise.

In the second of the terrible two, we find the affixed belief that God is against our being prosperous. But is that really the nature of God? Certain religious or social conditionings often make it difficult to discern the truth. And as we carry forward the theme of the undeserving, feelings of guilt, shame, and blame play a formidable role in how we curtail our expectation. Fortunately, an excellent resource to help dispel or counteract this misnomer is the Holy Bible. The "Good Book" contains many great stories, instances, and examples [often involving flawed people] that decry the cacophony of inherent error found within the belief that God is against one being prosperous.

In the 28th chapter of Deuteronomy, the writer explains how the blessings of the Lord can be experienced through our obedience. According to this scripture, everything from the towns and fields to the children and crops will be blessed. "Wherever you go and whatever you do will be blessed; the Lord will give you prosperity in the land." The writer makes the Lord seem awfully propitious. By these words, does it appear as though God is against prosperity? To be fair, the writer also lists the many curses that follow disobedience. But here, we are not debating the merits of obedience versus disobedience; rather, we are interested in identifying the precedent wherein God has already facilitated the flow of prosperity into the lives of God's children.

Proverbs 29:25 says, "Trusting the Lord leads to prosperity." In his book Prosperity, Charles Fillmore states, "Just thinking about God will draw to you the things you want and expect, and bring about many other blessings that you had not even thought about." The unfailing nature of God is such that to experience God's goodness is all the Father-Mother desires for us.

No provider or nurturer worth their parental salt hopes to see their offspring doing poorly. How much more then must the Creator of all good desire to see the offspring doing well? Jesus expressed it this way: "Is there anyone among you who, if your child asks for bread, will give a stone? Or if the child asks for a fish, will give a snake? Of course not! So if you who err know how to give good gifts to your children, how much more will your heavenly Father give good things to those who ask Him?"

Remember, it is God's good pleasure to give you the kingdom. If you have been holding on to a concept that has held you in a troubled space, it might be time to embrace a new reality. God is pro-you and pro-prosperity. Change your mind and discover how holistic and sensible a reality this really is.

The benefits of change are here, and ready to be realized. There is an abundant supply of prosperity and good. It might not always be easy to arrive at this conclusion, yet the difficulty at which it is arrived makes it no less real. The good news for each of us is that we have the mental capacity to change our present condition. The critical task is to know the Truth.

Depending upon what you study, you can always find evidence to support what it is you might be seeking to prove, but here are a few things to keep in mind. Through change, you can become equipped to manifest your prosperity. Through change, you can live the life you desire. Through change, you can uncover your talents, skills, crafts, gifts and abilities. Through change, you can open your creativity. And through change, you can discover a new you. Change is constant, so continue to unfold, evolve and emerge. The benefits of change are wonderful, and waiting for you.

Notes

_____

_____

_____

_____

_____

_____

_____

_____

_____

_____

_____

ABOUT THE AUTHOR

The Reverend Eric Ovid Donaldson has dedicated his life and his talents to the health and well-being of many of America's communities. A program developer, speaker, entrepreneur, a past Executive Director of a national nonprofit organization and a past President of an International Youth group, Rev. Donaldson is currently traveling across America conducting retreat-like spiritual weekend experiences simply called, "The Healing Workshop." The Healing Workshop has resulted in sustainable physical, mental, emotional and social healings that are documented in written, spoken and videotaped testimonies that are available on his website.

Contact:
Senior Minister
Unity Christian Church
3345 McCorkle Road
Memphis, TN 38116
901-461-3403
www.unitychristianchurch.us
www.thehealingministries.net
www.facebook.com/rev.donaldson
www.facebook.com/UnityChristianChurch
newthoughthealer@gmail.com

- Eleven -

The Perils of Hoarding Money

By Rev. Eric Ovid Donaldson

I began concentrating my thoughts on The Perils of Hoarding Money, knowing that as I did, examples of how I could best describe and explain the topic would soon appear. Like clockwork, the Universe supplied and did not disappoint.

After a long period on the road, facilitating Healing Workshop weekends around the country, I came home to my loving wife Valencia and our two children, Deja and Davon. When Daddy comes home we often celebrate by going to "China," as my two small children put it; we dine out at our favorite Chinese buffet. After eating to our hearts' content, the waiter brought the bill, appreciatively adorned with four fortune cookies. My children, sensing something sweet within range, grabbed at the cookies (leaving the bill untouched and intact). Then my wife took her cookie, lovingly leaving one for me. My children first ripped into the wrapping of the cookie each had chosen, then tore into

the cookie, leaving our table lightly dusted with crumbs. What they wanted were the fortunes inside the cookies.

"Read my fortune, Mommy," one said while I began to review the bill. My wife read the children's fortunes, and then read her own. Realizing there was one fortune cookie left, the children began to hone in on the prize. Knowing my children's enthusiasm for anything that turns out to be "the last one," I quickly picked up the cookie and began unwrapping it. The children crowded me, each wanting the privilege of reading the fortune for me as Mom had done for them. Being that they are in kindergarten and preschool, I thought better. Besides, for some reason, I wanted to read it myself. I'm glad I did, for the fortune was indeed for me:

A huge fortune at home is not as good as money in use.

I knew it was time to complete this chapter.

In many families around the world, the importance of saving is wisely stressed.

Whether it is for college or retirement, or Christmas, it is an admirable practice. Hoarding however, while resembling saving in some aspects, is not admirable at all. Many of us have heard news stories about the elderly man or woman who, when they died, was found hoarding thousands of dollars, while living in squalor. What would have someone live in this way unnecessarily? Are there deep-seated hurts or painful experiences that drive people to such irrational actions, or is it some sort of psychological disorder or disease? Are there sociological conditions that trigger this behavior, or is this behavior the expression of some sort of subconscious fear?

Profile of a Hoarder

Some of the characteristics that develop in a hoarder of money are as follows:

- **Hoarders of money seem to have difficulty discriminating between what is or will be the useful thing to do, and how best to use the money he has.**

147

A hoarder of money tends to experience unreasonable alarm when things seem to be dwindling or in short supply. We only have to watch those involved on Wall Street to observe this dynamic. US Congressman Jo Bonner of Alabama once said that at many points during our nation's history, there have been times—known in our history textbooks as "panics"—when adverse conditions affecting the financial and economic sectors of the country have caused individuals to hoard more than they need. If this perspective is true, then hoarding seems to be initiated by some difficult or undesirable circumstances, which is then followed by some fear-based reaction: a panic, anxiety or apprehension.

- **Hoarders of money are often reacting to a past hurt, experience or transgression and as a result, are greatly concerned about the future.**

The current circumstance or condition the hoarder faces triggers the trauma of the past experience: an experience that compelled the hoarder to reach a deep-seated conclusion about people, about life. A compulsion toward protection emerges, and the hoarder digs in, doing whatever is necessary to keep to one's self as well as keep things to one's self. Few, if any can be trusted. British mathematician Isaac Barrow once said that because men believe (trust) not in Providence, they do so greedily scrape and hoard. They do not believe in any reward for charity, therefore they will part with nothing.

- **Many hoarders of money are also recluses, bound by the very thing he/she is hoarding.**

  It is interesting that another definition for the word "hoarding" describes it as a fence, barrier, or cover, enclosing, surrounding, or concealing something. It's indicative of what happens to the hoarder, not just the hoarded. When seeing these symptoms in operation within the context of money, an interesting dynamic comes into view. We will explore this dynamic later on in the chapter.

To simply focus on hoarding as only the compulsive acquisition of things is to miss the crucial and ironic consequence and peril. While hoarding gives one a sense of attaining wealth, the items attained are never available for appraisal or sale. The item's value and its condition deteriorate and eventually become worthless. The compulsive acquiring of things is what leads to an act of hoarding, but hoarding itself involves the obsessive possessing of those things. Hoarding, therefore, is the improvident burying of oneself within one's possessions.

The Parable of the Talents

Allegorically and metaphysically The Parable of the Talents found in the Holy Bible is a sound study of the dangers of hoarding money (Matt. 25:14–30 NRSV). Each verse helps us understand simple truths surrounding the nuances of money management (or the lack thereof). Obviously, this isn't what Jesus was actually discussing (he was actually describing the kingdom of heaven), but his analogy works because people relate to the truth in the story he tells to make his point.

In this parable, Jesus masterfully teaches his listeners from simple everyday scenarios that provide a greater understanding of the nature of the Kingdom of Heaven. Jesus' teachings not only describe the Kingdom of Heaven, but also include images of the "perils" of hell: weeping, darkness, gnashing of the teeth. It's important to note that Jesus believed that the Kingdom of God is in the midst of each of us (Luke 17:21), perhaps as a state of mind that results in an experience. To Jesus, the Kingdom is not a place, nor can it be readily observed.

In this particular parable, the Kingdom of Heaven is symbolized by a man with servants. The servants represent the listener, both those listening to Jesus as well as ourselves, the listener of the scripture. The talents provided by the man is money or symbolically, something that is meant to be used to sustain ourselves and grow. Each servant is given an amount based on their ability (varying degrees of consciousness).

I find it interesting that Jesus would choose a man with servants to describe the Kingdom of Heaven. He is not saying that there are slaves or servants in heaven. Jesus is actually describing the dynamic of our relationship to this Kingdom. We are all subject to spiritual laws as spiritual beings. This realm of divine ideas called heaven provides what is needed for us to be productive and to have fruitful, healthy experiences. It matters not what you begin with; the talent has value. Still, more important than the value of the talent is how the talent is used by its possessor.

In the parable, the servant given five talents and the servant given two talents do business with their talents and double their talents in the process. The message is clear. When we use what we have been given responsibly, we reap benefits. In fact, the man, upon seeing his servants' success, empowers them with more responsibility. *For unto whomsoever much is given, of him shall be much required....* (Luke 12:48). An inherent sense of accomplishment and fulfillment is experienced as both are invited to enter into the joy of their master: enter into the joy of heaven. However, not everyone succeeds in the story. The servant who was given one talent makes a terrible mistake; he hoards his talent, which begins a perilous deterioration. Several points and principles can be taken from this servant's actions as well.

Points of Peril

Perilous Point Number 1: Never Burying Your Talent. Money is a medium of exchange. When money is hoarded, whether it is buried, squirreled away or squandered, it is not involved in the purpose for which it was created. We plant things we intend to grow, and we bury things we see as dead or no longer useful. A thing's value is determined by its usefulness. Hoarding money is a spiritual and a social divestiture; it is a liquidation of faith, and a stagnation of utility. The servant given one talent is involved in an act of disrespect and irresponsibility toward the master (heaven), unappreciative of the opportunity successfully taken by the other two servants.

Perilous Point Number 2: Hoarding Brings Disorder. Nothing hoarded is ever orderly. Whether it's money in a mattress, or buried in the backyard, hoarding is never an orderly act. Anything hoarded eventually becomes messy, plain and simple. Hoarding results in clutter followed by dysfunction. The servant, being out of order in the use of his talent, creates disorder in his hoarding and in his life. He is out of order with his master (the lord or law of his life) and the consequence is forthcoming (loss of his talent and aggravation). The servant is not invited into the joy of the Kingdom. In fact, he is stripped of what he has, deemed worthless, and thrown into outer darkness (a lifeless state of exclusion). Hoarding money results in deep frustration and unsound financial and life practices.

Perilous Point Number 3: Those Who Hoard Are Operating Out of Fear. The servant with the one talent shows his mindset. "Master, I knew that you were a harsh man," he says as he is explaining why he was unable to produce anything with his talent (Matthew 25:24). "I was afraid," he tells us as he returns the talent he had. A fearful mindset first paralyzes the person's thinking, then, in that state of duress, plunges them into detrimental and non-productive reactions. There is no faith operating in one's life when one hoards. Everything is predicated on (harsh) preconceived notions about the source of the talent. Hoarders often believe (or conclude) that life is harsh or heaven is hard to come by. A spiritual inertia results. The laws of increase are never enacted. In fact, the hoarder shuts down and literally packs it in.

Move Past the Perils of Hoarding Money

Moving past the perils of hoarding money requires the fostering of a healthy attitude toward money. A healthy attitude comes from an even healthier understanding of money's purpose, and how best to use money toward living an abundant life.

Religiously speaking, many people's attitudes toward money stem from the interpretation of one scripture:

> For the love of money is a root of all kinds of evil...
> — I Timothy 6:10 NRSV

This one piece of scripture (often mentioned and taken out of both its scriptural and historical context) is responsible for many misunderstandings around money.

If this scripture is properly understood and seen in its spiritual perspective, it can go a long way toward avoiding the perils of hoarding money. Simply put, it is not the money, but the *love of* (obsession over) money that is a root of all kinds of evil. Jesus tells us to "Strive first for the Kingdom of God and His righteousness, and all these things will be given to you as well" (Matthew 6:33). Jesus is imploring us to faithfully seek first an understanding of the realm of Spirit (the Kingdom of God) and its orderly laws for living abundantly (righteousness), then all the things we strive for materially will be provided for (as well), without losing our minds (or our soul), which is the evil we seek to avoid. *For what shall it profit a man, if he shall gain (hoard) the whole world, and lose his own soul (Mark 8:36)?*

This is the beauty of following Jesus' approach. No one wants to experience anything that is adverse to life and living (evil). But that is what happens when we fail to cultivate a proper perspective on money and possessions. Faithfully developing a healthy attitude toward money by getting a greater understanding of these universally spiritual principles taught by Jesus and others will help us to properly possess our possessions in a manner that serves, and not hinders. Falling into the perils of hoarding money, however, will always result in our possessions possessing us.

References

1. Langley Collyer: The Mystery Hoarder of Harlem; http://www.ocfoundation.info/hoarding/case-studies/langley-collyer-the-mystery-hoarder-of-harlem. php; copyright 2006–2009, International OCD Foundation, all rights reserved.

2. Dante, The Divine Comedy; pp. 67–73; translated by A.S. Kline. Illustrated Edition; copyright 2000 A.S. Kline, all rights reserved.

Notes

_____

_____

_____

_____

_____

_____

_____

_____

_____

About The Author

The Reverend Bernette Lee Jones is the senior minister at the One God One Thought Center in Baltimore, Maryland; a member church of the Universal Foundation for Better Living , founded by the Reverend Dr. Johnnie Colemon. Her work in New Thought Christian ministry includes developing a greater consciousness for Spirit driven leadership ; the inspiration and development of spiritual, transformational leaders, able to take their rightful place, doing God's business in the world. She has mentored, coached, supported, spiritually guided and taught spiritual leaders in ministries, community based organizations, and small businesses. In addition to being a writer, she has also presented nationally as a keynote speaker, seminar, retreat and workshop leader. Reverend Bernette's emerging model for personal transformation, called "Conscious Life Design Systems", has been used by many as a simple living system to put their life in order based on timeless spiritual principles that have proven to be both powerful and effective. Her recent release" Drive Time :Affirmations, Prayers and Soul Beats " has been acknowledged by many as a dynamic and unique consciousness raising tool that makes their car a " riding sanctuary."

Reverend Bernette is a member of the national boards of the Universal Foundation for Better Living and the International New Thought Alliance (INTA).

Rev. Bernette L. Jones

One God One Thought Center for Better Living

3605 Coronado Road.

Baltimore, Maryland 21244

410.496.5188

www.ogot.org

bjones927@aol.com

- Twelve -
The Power of
Your Habits

By Rev. Bernette Lee Jones

The cab driver taking me to the airport in Fort Lauderdale was apparently smitten. As the drive progressed, I learned why when he told me of his recent experiences with sadness yet hope. He was a Haitian who had lost everything material in the 2009 hurricane, so he and his wife moved to the United States to start over. Now, he was facing the fact that his children and other family members, who were still in Haiti, might not still be alive after the earthquake on January 12, 2010.

Hearing this, I thought, *God, by the fresh anointing of your Holy Spirit, comfort him and all those who are sharing this experience, so that they know how to get through and emerge even stronger. Reveal to his heart and soul a new thought and a new awareness that every ending is a new beginning and every new beginning is a fresh anointing, because God is right here and God is also right there in Haiti.*

My heart opened and I spoke little. Respecting that this was not the time to be preachy or even attempt to "metafizzle" the topic at hand, I let him talk and I was there for him, being present in the best way I knew how: praying without ceasing.

What struck me about his attitude, even while dealing through the obvious pain of not being able to get a call through or know the status of his loved ones, was his sense of quiet strength that emerged in exceptionally interesting ways. When I first got into the cab, before hearing his story, I had asked, "How much is the ride from the hotel to the airport?" He simply said, "You can afford it, you have enough." I knew his affirmation was true and I agreed with him rather than listening to my mind-chatter that tried to get my attention, saying, *How does he know what I can afford?*

In that moment, I knew we both knew the Truth. Even in the face of his seemingly catastrophic, horrific experience and my trite concern about cab fare rates, in that moment we knew the Truth with and for each other. And in reality, it was all the same. An all-powerful, all-mighty, all-loving, all-gracious, all-merciful God knows no difference between a level #1 or a level #12 on our human consciousness scale. It is our faith in the awareness that God is the infinite source and common thread of omnipresence through it all. That gets us through it all.

At the end of our encounter and journey together, I gave him a generous tip, way beyond the total of the cab fare. It felt like the right thing to do. He looked at me and smiled warmly, saying, "You see, I knew that you would have more than enough." I blessed him and verbally affirmed God's life, love, peace and prosperity for him, his family and everyone in Haiti. He thanked me for the prayers and the tip. I knew in my heart that he and his wife would be able to deal with whatever the new circumstances presented. His strength to think, feel and know "More than enough" would sustain and prosper them on their journey.

Habits of Thinking & Feeling

> Habits … thousands of small acts and restraints
> over time.
>
> — Author Unknown

Prosperity is generated in our habits of thinking, feeling, believing and knowing, in a confident way, that God is, right now, more than enough, more than sufficient, for all we could ever need or require. This also means we are more than enough as we recognize, accept and realize we are made in the image likeness of God. We are capable and able to respond in any situation we might encounter by knowing that the substance of our God consciousness can be converted into whatever material form we seem to require. We cannot practice thinking and feeling that something is missing or lacking and, at the same time, expect to experience a divine flow. In God, by Its very nature, it is not possible for anything to be either missing or lacking.

Prosperity is a habit of knowing and feeling that we are safe, well and provided for, and unfolding spiritually, mentally, emotionally and physically at the right pace and growing all the time. We know in our soul that this feeling of security is the principle Truth that allows us to draw to us and to take in God's infinite ideas. Prosperity is a habit of consistently, consciously practicing the kinds of thinking and feeling that builds the awareness within us that there is "more than enough" at all times, regardless of physical evidence that may seem contrary. God has already "godded" us with consciousness that is providing what we are, what we have, and what we are doing. If we are in the habit of thinking that who we are, what we have and what we are doing is not enough, it is based in an unconscious moment that somehow the infinite, ever-expanding, inexhaustible source, the Omnipresence we call God, has become limited or is withholding something from us.

It was so clear to me, from my brief but profound exchange with my Haitian friend, that who we are being in every moment is shaped by our habits of thought and feeling. Regardless of the apparent prevailing circumstances, by cultivating prosperous habits of mind, prosperity prevails by giving us the stamina and fortitude to persist until we can see the outer evidence of prosperity. I was impressed that my Haitian friend was not in the habit of focusing on doom and gloom, having a pity party, or even asking for sympathy. Here he was with an obvious life experience that seemed too catastrophic to even imagine, and he was affirming me. He was in the habit consciousness of affirming "more than enough." This habit of being and thinking kicked in automatically in a genuine and authentic way, demonstrating that our inner habits are powerful in shaping our outer experiences. I noticed the impact of his attitude on me. I received and was moved by his affirmation and smile in the face of obvious challenges that could have left him bitter and cold. He received my prayers and a portion of my tithe.

Habits of thinking and feeling have a powerful impact. They

are repeated so often they become the routine wallpaper in the background of our consciousness. Our conscious or unconscious habits of thinking and feeling eventually display themselves in manifested forms within the day-to-day experiences of our lives. Collectively, they turn into belief systems. Belief systems put us on automatic pilot and are the operating systems that produce repeating patterns of experiences. Too often, we are unaware we might be in the habit of unconsciously perceiving lack and limitation in the face of an abundant and forever-expanding universe.

Prosperity might well be lurking within our daily routine experiences, as mundane as they may seem, when we take a closer look at our inner habits. The power of our routine habits is that they are the building blocks of consciousness and character. We might discover that good, intentional inner habits of mind can spark an abundance of new thoughts, new awareness, new ideas, new interests and even new sources of income. Prosperity lives in the joy of the present moment when we are willing to practice inner habits of giving our attention to the presence of God, choosing to think rightly about ourselves, and making commitments to give and serve others.

The Habit of Attention

> For where your treasure is, there your heart
> will be also.
> — Matthew 6:21 NRSV

"Understanding and managing attention is now the single most important determinant of business success"; "Attention is the real currency of business and individuals." " Arguably, "attention has become a more valuable currency than the kind you store in bank ac counts." Our attention allows us to make "the decisions and actions necessary to make the world better."
— The Attention Economy by T. Davenport & J. Beck

Managing our attention is one of the most important inner habits that we can develop as we make strides toward a more prosperous life. Mastering our own attention is treasuring the value of our own attention in mastering our own mind. Nowadays, everybody has a personal screen of some sort to manage their outer attention. People want to view, stay connected and interact with the world outside. There are screens for entertainment, screens for communication, screens for obtaining information, screens for seeing what is happening on the other side of the world. We might ask ourselves, are we managing the screens or are the screens managing us?

What gets our attention also gets our time, our money, and our priority. But far more important than all of that, what gets our attention gets to settle into our subconscious mind, our heart, and according to spiritual principle, will eventually display itself on the big screen that tells our life stories. Attention is habit forming. Understanding the power and impact of habits, we would do well to guard our precious attention from the distractions that take us in the opposite direction from where we think we are headed. There is prospering power in cultivating the habit of an attentive mind. We have the ability to notice, on the inner screen of our mind, what has our attention, and to decide whether what we are focusing our attention upon will give us the power to shift directions to think, feel and be more prosperous.

When dealing with a financial challenge, are we in the habit of giving our attention to God's new ideas for increased revenue streams, or do we focus on debt or overdrafts and how stressed we are from grappling with problems? When dealing with a health challenge, do we give attention to the principle of life, the healing power of God, and appreciate moments of wellness, or do we focus on making sure that everybody we know knows how bad we feel and everything the doctor says is wrong with us?

In the foreword to his book *Prosperity*, Charles Fillmore writes that what we need to realize above all else is that God has provided for the most minute needs of our daily lives, and if we lack anything it is because we have not used our minds in making the right connection with Source. Cultivating the habit of pausing on a regular basis to give God our undivided attention results in a divine richness and luster in our consciousness, character and countenance. The more attention we give to God and the spiritual disciplines of meditation, prayer and study, the more we gain in spiritual understanding, inspiration, guidance, renewed energy and vitality. Attention to God anchors our consciousness in the infinite source of all that is, so that we are aware of our wholeness. It unfolds a process of thinking and feeling that provides stability, balance and order in our lives. As we choose to give attention to wholeness, rather than brokenness, we experience the feelings of well-being, empowerment and fulfillment that prompt us to take bold actions that lead to outcomes we might have never before imagined we were capable of accomplishing.

The Habit of Choice

> Choose this day whom you will serve ... as for me
> and my household, we will serve the Lord
> — Joshua 24:15

As conscious beings, we have the freewill power to choose to think and believe whatever we choose to think and believe about God, ourselves, other people, what we do, and the context or community in which we participate. The habit of choice is the habit of stopping our mind chatter long enough to consciously select our thoughts and feelings rather than merely reacting to what the outward circumstances might suggest. The habit of choice or conscious selection means that we slow down to be mindful of the eventual outcomes that will result from our inner choices in the present moment. We choose to take time and make time to connect to God before we make decisions. Knowing this principle, we are more inclined to choose wisely this day who we will serve in our selected thoughts, feelings, words, actions and reactions. Will we choose to serve lack, the appearance of not enough, or will we choose to serve all sufficiency, more than enough of anything required? Each moment of our choice is pivotal and significant.

Charles Fillmore also often reminded us in his classic works that "right identification," how we choose to identify ourselves, is the first and most important mind process for establishing the habit of accepting and embracing ourselves as prosperous beings. Being in the habit of choosing to identify ourselves as the offspring of God, we recognize that our true parentage and heritage is spiritual in nature rather than human in nature. This self-conception as a child of God is also the claim to our divine inheritance of an inexhaustible supply. Being in the habit of thinking about ourselves as a prospering child of God and feeling prosperous helps us to uncover and recognize that abundance and prosperity is happening in our lives right now and at all times. The ability to discern abundance and to appreciate its presence comes with spiritual understanding. Thinking and feeling prosperous is an inner habit of choice that is not based on any outer evidence. It is a choice based totally on the awareness that since God's abundance is present and available everywhere, at all times, we can choose to consciously identify ourselves as prosperous.

We already have everything within us that is required for us to grow abundantly in every area of life. As we develop the habit of choosing to give our attention to God, we become more

168

consciousness of how to attract and tap into ideas, resources, creative financing, enjoyable relationships, surprise gifts, and miraculous encounters with just the right people. Numerous books and personal testimonies from those who have endured and overcome incredible challenges in life let us know that it is absolutely possible to go from wherever we think we are right now, whether financially, in relationships, in finding our divine right job, business or home, to wherever we think we would like to be. No matter where we are, it is possible to get there from here. But first, we must be able to get there in our consciousness. "Seek first the kingdom of God and all these things will be added" (Matthew 6:33). We don't have to use outer efforts to "make" or "force" ourselves to become some way that we "should," "ought" or "have" to be according to outside standards. It is not necessary to manipulate, scheme or contrive in the outer physical world of people and effects.

The Habit of Commitment

We mistakenly believe that prosperity is demonstrated when we receive—when money comes to us or we get a new job. This is not true. Prosperity's demonstration is giving.

— *Even Mystics Have Bills to Pay, by Jim Rosemergy*

Staying consciously in the divine flow of abundance and prosperity requires that we develop the habit of commitment, which is demonstrated in the practices of giving and receiving. Commitment is the inner habit that establishes a certain level of consistency in outward practices of service that is reliable and dependable. We place ourselves in a covenant relationship with God to be part of God's distribution system on the earth in all the ways and areas we serve: whether it be at home, in community, on the job, in business or in spiritual community.

The habit of commitment makes it certain that God has a definite place to express fluently all the life, wisdom, love, power and substance that makes up the absolute good of God's nature. Our consciousness of the principles that express through these five attributes of God is our true prosperity. As we allow God to express through us, we are serving all humanity in that, as our way-shower Christ Jesus has taught us, what any one of us demonstrates we can be and do, we all can be and do. We are prospered with ongoing health and wellness when we have the consciousness that God is expressing the principle of life through us and through all people everywhere. We are prospered with ongoing financial security when we have the consciousness that God is expressing the principle of substance through us and through all people everywhere. We are prospered with ongoing kindness, cooperation, forgiveness and harmonious relationships when we have the consciousness that God is expressing the principle of love through us and through all people everywhere. We are prospered when we know the same principle is omnipresent, and is available and working for and within all people everywhere. This consciousness is part of our loving service to humanity.

We live our commitment when we practice the habits of consistent, joyful giving of our spiritual gifts, financial tithes and creative ideas. Through our contributions we become open channels that are stronger and more sturdy, with the ability to handle greater and greater affluence in the "currency of God," which is Christ consciousness. Whenever there seems to be a need, our first response must be to get into the habit of giving. The Reverend Dr. Johnnie Colemon used to say that "when her money started looking funny," she would start giving to restart the flow. She taught us that there is never a time when we cannot find some way to start the giving flow, which in turn will open the way to the receiving of whatever we seem to need.

References

    Holy Bible (New Revised Standard Version)

    The Attention Economy by Thomas H. Davenport and John S. Beck

    Prosperity by Charles Fillmore

    Even Mystics Have Bills to Pay by Jim Rosemergy

    Lessons in Truth by H. Emilie Cady

    It Works If You Work It by Reverend Dr. Johnnie Colemon

Notes

Thirteen

The Importance of Budgeting

By Robert Henderson Jr. CFP ®

Yes, yes, yes, I know, for some of you reading about the importance of a budget is as about exciting as watching paint dry, and yes, I totally understand where you are coming from. But before you blow past this lesson without giving it a second chance, please allow me to present this lesson from a whole new, different viewpoint. Now, unless you have a machine that prints real money (not counterfeit) or you just happen to own a goose that lays golden eggs, you really do need to understand the importance of a budget. Many people take this lesson for granted, but trust me, it is an integral part of becoming financially sound. In fact, it reminds me of one of the most important Laws of the Universe, and that law is the law of Order. Anything and everything that has worth and substance begins with Order. There is order in the universe; therefore there must be order in your life and affairs. Without "Order" your life as well as your business will be filled with chaos. Many people have failed to realize or understand the importance of this law and as a result, continue to fail at almost every financial endeavor they pursue. Order is the first law, just as establishing and following a budget is the first rule for operating a business correctly. The same applies to getting one's personal financial affairs in order. There are countless people from all walks of life who feel that as long as they're making lots of money, they don't need a budget. Time has revealed that anyone who has ever adopted this way of thinking has often found themselves a day late and a dollar

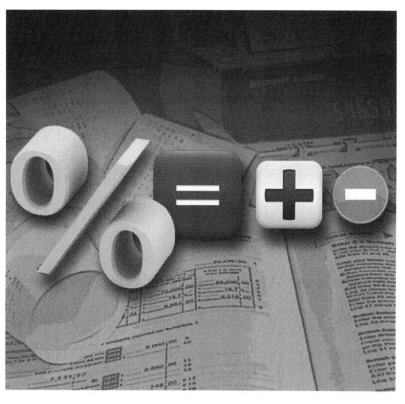

short of meeting their goals and objectives. You see, a budget is sort of like a gage; in fact, it is a gage. Its purpose is to give you specific information to be able to perform a certain task. How well would a pilot operate an aircraft without the use of his gages or how far could a scuba diver descending deep into the ocean without the use of an oxygen gage. When you think about it honestly, we all need some sort of gage, and when it comes to money and finances, a budget represents that gage. One of the benefits of a budget is, it takes the human element (emotion) out of making business decisions and deals strictly with the facts. If done correctly, a budget will never lie or deceive you. In other words, a budget is the best pure financial friend that you could ever have; it will tell you the truth even when you don't want to know the truth. A friend might tell you what they think, but a budget will tell you what you need to know. There's a saying in the business world that says "men may lie, women may lie, but numbers don't"; a rapper said it in a song also. My goal in this lesson is to get you the reader, to begin to repent. In other words, think a new thought and learn to respect the power of a budget in not only your business life, but your personal life and affairs as well. I know it sounds redundant, but, being redundant is required in order to break old habits. I can't stress to you enough how so many people try to develop a plan for saving and investing without first instituting a sound budget. The word budget is often used when dealing in the financial world. Now don't get me wrong, I know reading all this is easier said than done. But if you truly want to be successful, you have to learn, to make yourself, do all the things, that you know you ought to do, when you don't feel like doing them. Wow! Make sure you read that again. Remember, this is a lesson and lessons are meant to be studied not just read. In order to get this right, it's going to require you to brush-up on strengthening your will power as well as self-discipline. As you begin to grow more in consciousness, you'll notice that words like will power, self-discipline, faith, imagination are all closely related to each other. Actually the word budget is a cousin to the word balance. In the world of accounting, you've often heard the term "checks and balance" and even if you're not an accounting major, I'm sure you've heard all the fuss about balancing America's budget. Basically, America has been spending more money than it has. In other words, America is out of balance and there is a problem with its budget. Once the problem is acknowledged, the proper steps must be taken in order to avoid future problems that often lead to becoming bankrupt. Again, as you can see, budget and balance are very much related to each. Adhering to a sound budget will automatically bring balance in your life and affairs. Take your health for example, doctors tell many of us we are overweight according to our height and body structure. A man who is 5 ft. tall and weighs 300 pounds is said to not only be overweight, but out of balance as well. It won't be long before the extra weight begins to take a toll on his back and other parts of his body as well as his internal organs. Being out of budget and therefore, out of balance is an accident waiting to happen. Think for a moment and let's use your imagination. Imagine yourself getting ready to take a road trip and driving your car from Florida to California. Do you just jump in your car spontaneously and drive away heading west? Or do you at least give some thought to the physical and mechanical condition of your vehicle and its ability to get you to your destination without any problems. Or maybe, you decide it's much better to rent a car rather than put the wear and tear and mileage on your personal vehicle. You'd also have to consider the cost of the road trip and whether you could afford to rent a vehicle or if it would be more cost effective to drive your own car. What about gas and food consumption? How much will it cost? Even if you use an electric car and pack your own food, you'll still have some expenses that need to be figured into the cost of your road trip. My point here is, if you plan on completing and having a successful road trip, you'll need to plan, create and follow a budget in order to insure a successful trip. If your budget is small and you have a minimal amount of money, creating and understanding how to work within your budget will keep you from living beyond your means like renting a limousine and hiring a personal driver when you can't afford to. Again, as I stated earlier, a good budget gives you specific information, it tells you what you can and cannot afford to do. If you have a business, a good budget will tell you when you can afford to hire as well as how much you can afford to pay your staff as well as how much you can afford to pay yourself. It will also tell you how much money you need to sell your goods and services for in order to turn a profit. As you can see, a budget tells you many things. Remember what I said earlier, the old saying about a budget, "the numbers don't lie". A budget will reveal if there is any money left over and available for discretionary pending after overhead expenses are paid. This is true regardless if the budget is for a business or for personal use, the end result is the same, either a positive or negative cash flow will emerge. It's sad, but true, that 75 percent of people have never use or established a personal budget. No wonder many people are living paycheck to paycheck and struggling to make ends meet. Stop making excuses by saying there isn't enough money; the problem is the majority of people are living beyond their means. In other words, spending what we don't have by over using credit cards. We can't continue to go through life sort of like someone taking a road trip with a broken gas gage and limited amounts of financial resources; letting chance and circumstance control and direct our lives. Anytime you allow this to happen, it is said that you are out of harmony with your true self. Listen, life is about learning, learning who you are and discovering your purpose in this life. On the next few pages I have provided a sample of a basic personal budget. Use it as a guide to help you establish a personal budget. Make adjustments to the form to meet your personal situation as needed. The goal here is to be able to look at all your resources (money) that's coming in (inflow) and money that's going out (outflow) this will help you to begin to track your money. Looking at where and how you spend your money on paper in black and white has been known to work wonders on the human mind. Most people are shocked to find out just how much they spend on lunch in a month. Establishing a budget for you and your family will help you in more ways than one. In today's world, where everything is moving so fast and change is happening all around us, it's good to step back and take a look at yourself, outside of yourself to recognize not only where you are, but more so, where you're headed. It's a wonderful thing. A budget will help you see the truth. Happy New You!

CASH FLOW WORKSHEET		
CATEGORY	MONTHLY	ANNUALLY
INCOME:		
Wages and Bonuses		
Interest Income		
Investment Income		
Miscellaneous Income		
Income Subtotal		
INCOME TAXES WITHHELD:		
Federal Income Tax		
State and Local Income Tax		
Social Security/Medicare Tax		
Income Taxes Subtotal		
Spendable Income		
EXPENSES:		
HOME:		
Mortgage or Rent		
Homeowners/Renters Insurance		
Property Taxes		
Home Repairs/Maintenance/HOA Dues		
Home Improvements		
UTILITIES:		
Electricity		
Water and Sewer		
Natural Gas or Oil		
Telephone (Land Line, Cell)		
FOOD:		
Groceries		
Eating Out, Lunches, Snacks		
FAMILY OBLIGATIONS:		
Child Support/Alimony		
Day Care, Babysitting		
HEALTH AND MEDICAL:		
Insurance (Life & Medical)		
Out-of-Pocket Medical Expenses		
Fitness (Yoga,Massage,Gym)		

The Henderson Financial Group, Inc.
5783A NW 151st Street I Miami Lakes, FL 33014
Ph: 305-825-1444 I Fax: 786-230-8392

CASH FLOW WORKSHEET		
CATEGORY	**MONTHLY**	**ANNUALLY**
TRANSPORTATION:		
Car Payments		
Gasoline/Oil		
Auto Repairs/Maintenance/Fees		
Auto Insurance		
Other (tolls, bus, subway, taxi)		
DEBT PAYMENTS:		
Credit Cards		
Student Loans		
Other Loans		
ENTERTAINMENT/RECREATION:		
Cable TV/Videos/Movies		
Computer Expense		
Hobbies		
Subscriptions and Dues		
Vacations		
PETS:		
Food		
Grooming, Boarding, Vet		
CLOTHING:		
INVESTMENTS AND SAVINGS:		
401(K)or IRA		
Stocks/Bonds/Mutual Funds		
College Fund		
Savings		
MISCELLANEOUS:		
Toiletries, Household Products		
Church Tithes & Offering		
Charitable Donations		
Grooming (Hair, Make-up, Other)		
Miscellaneous Expense		
Total Investments and Expenses		
Surplus/Shortage (Spendable income minus expenses & investments)		

The Henderson Financial Group, Inc.
5783A NW 151st Street ┆ Miami Lakes, FL 33014
Ph: 305-825-1444 ┆ Fax: 786-230-8392

Notes

_____

_____

_____

_____

_____

_____

_____

_____

_____

_____

_____

Fourteen

The Power of the Subconscious Mind

By The Rev. Evan Reid

The eye is the lamp of the body; if your eye is sound,
your whole body will be full of light.

Man operates out of one's mind and in order for us to
understand how it works, we might compartmentalize it. We might

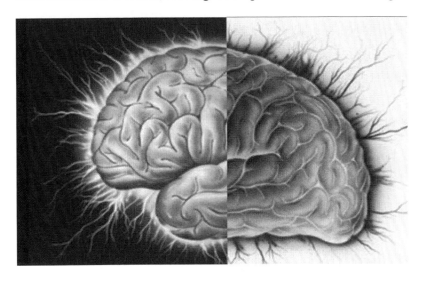

say that there are three phases of mind: the Super-conscious, the Conscious and the Subconscious.

The *Super-conscious phase* is the segment of mind referred to as the spiritual center of the soul from and through which we commune with the Universal Source. It holds the true nature of our being; it is also referred to as the Christ mind: the perfect pattern of God in man or spiritual man whom the Creator God of Genesis made.

There is the *Conscious phase*, which is also described as the creative imagination, the area of awareness that operates in the now. It is through this phase that we are able to observe, perceive, transform and translate ideas; the pixels of energy that surround us and operate through the capacity to think; the shaping and forming of these invisible fundamental building blocks. In the conscious phase of mind we are able to analyze, justify and make decisions.

The other area of the mind is termed the *Subconscious phase.* This area might be viewed as both a storehouse and incubator of all the thought seeds that flow from the conscious segment. It has no formative ability; its power is in its ability to store and manifest without altering whatever it receives. The law that governs it is belief.

When thoughts are developed in the conscious phase and the decision to accept them is made, they are clothed with emotion; good or bad connotations then find their way to the subconscious where they are held and expanded. Thoughts are equivalent to seeds, and the subconscious is the environment in which these thought seeds are planted and where they expand. When thoughts are accepted and proven through experience, they are held as truths and form the basis for beliefs from which all expression—words, actions and reactions and experiences—are drawn forth. Beliefs are individualized truth, hence subjective. They are definitely not absolute. They are opinions based on the way one has programmed one's mind to be able to translate and interpret the spiritual information that is everywhere present. These programs are held in the Subconscious. Each person is uniquely placed in the universe, and as a result sees everything differently, for no two persons can occupy the same space at the same time.

Over time the subconscious becomes one's frame of reference, for it holds the individual's history of experience and the many ways an individual has dealt with many situations and the ways he or she has resolved them. As a result, one conditions oneself to judge: to see in a particular way and come to conclusions. When Jesus was giving his recipe for experiencing the fullness of the kingdom, in Matthew 7:1, 2, he said, "Judge not, that you be not judged. For the judgment you pronounce you will be judged, and the measure you give will be the measure you get"—the way one trains oneself to see the outer results in the manner one experiences the outer and is affected by it. This is so, for we live out of the subconscious. "It is not what goes in that defiles the man but that which comes out." Everything that enters the mind is perfect but becomes imperfect through thinking, and the subconscious expresses the likeness. As a result, no expression that emerges from it is infallible. This holds true for pope to pauper. Nothing that comes from the "heart," the subconscious, is foolproof. The subconscious acts as the "eye" through which we view and interpret all spiritual essence that surrounds us, and we project our personal kaleidoscope unto the universe through the subconscious.

In the second chapter of Genesis, the writers and translators present us with an allegory that seeks to explain the development of mind. In the beginning there is One Power and One Presence, and out of this essence everything is shaped and formed. The last of the creation is man, who is patterned after the nature of this Active Creative Spirit. The first man is the super-conscious phase, the spiritual essence of our being having all the qualities of its author.

"Then the Lord God formed man out of the dust from the ground, and breathed into his nostrils the breath of life; and man became a living being" (Genesis 2:7). This might be looked at as the development of the conscious phase of mind, or the ability to think, to shape and form the universal everywhere present substance. The Lord God, Jehovah, refers to the super-conscious phase of mind or the Christ mind—the only-begotten expression of the universal Creator.

"And the Lord God planted a garden in Eden, in the east; and there He put the man whom He had formed. And out of the ground the Lord God made to grow every tree that is pleasant to the sight and good for food, the tree of life also in the midst of the garden, and the tree of knowledge of good and evil" (Genesis 2:8–9). The planting of the garden is the awakening of consciousness, the ability to perceive, observe, translate and transform universal substance. In part of the allegory there is also the ability to clothe everything with emotion, good and evil. Super-conscious mind instructs the conscious not to clothe thought patterns, the products of the conscious, with any form of emotion, but to accept everything it beholds in the manner it was created: perfect. This is crucial as the mind continues to develop.

"Then the Lord God said, 'It is not good that the man should be alone; I will make him a helper fit for him.' So out of the ground the Lord God formed every beast of the field and every bird of the air, and brought them to the man to see what he would call them; and whatever the man called every living creature, that was its name. The man gave names to all cattle, and to the birds of the air, and to every beast of the field; but for the man there was not found a helper fit for him.

"So the Lord God caused a deep sleep to fall upon the man, and while he slept took one of his ribs and closed up its place with flesh; and the rib which the Lord God had taken from the man He made into a woman and brought her to the man. Then the man said, 'This at last is bone of my bones and flesh of my flesh; she shall be called Woman, because she was taken out of Man'" (Genesis 2:18–23).

187

The woman or helpmate represents the subconscious. It is to help the conscious appreciate and appropriate the divine flow of the creative presence that surrounds him. It is not intended to lead the conscious, but to aid it by storing and giving birth to its desires.

The subconscious can be viewed as the place in mind out of which all of man's experiences are born. "Out of the heart come forth the issues of life." It is also where we bury all that passes through the conscious. "Except a grain of wheat falls into the earth and dies, it remains alone; but it dies, it bears much fruit" (John 12:24).

If one allows the conscious to be fed by the super-conscious, and all that is received is held in its perfect state and this is then fed into the subconscious, the fruits produced will be perfected. The conscious phase has become pivotal, and does not only rely on the Christ mind for its supply. It also draws from the stimuli it receives from the outer through the awaking of the five senses. It also depends on the regurgitated information it has stored in the subconscious, its helpmate, because if the seeds held in the subconscious are tainted, it receives spoiled fruit.

Again we go to Genesis 3: "Now the serpent was more subtle than any other wild creature that the Lord God had made. He said to the woman, 'Did God say you should not eat of any of the fruit of the garden?' and the woman said to the serpent 'We may eat of the fruits of the garden,' but God said, "You shall not eat of the fruit of the tree which is in the midst of the garden neither shall you touch it, lest you die."' But the serpent said to the woman, 'You shall not die.'"

There are three points to be touched on here.

1. Within man's consciousness are all the trees and animals, beasts, birds of the air, which represent ideas of all nature. Man, the conscious phase of mind, is able to use all these ideas, but not those that come good and evil: emotion. When we think, we will automatically attach an emotion or a nature to the thoughts produced and these go to the storehouse, the woman.

2. The serpent is part of man's consciousness and not an outside force that takes up residence. Its function is to provide us with opportunity to follow the instructions that come from super-conscious mind. If we follow its direction, it gains the ability to usurp the power of the super-conscious, and the ego or the "devil" of the New Testament grows.

3. The subconscious should be used purely for storage and the reproduction of our desires. Because the material it holds is drawn from past experiences and also because each moment affords us the opportunity to see and appreciate the universal flow of divine substance differently, it cannot be relied upon to direct us to new experiences. We must train

ourselves to be directed from our Christ self. When and where the subconscious rules, one will experience sameness and fall from grace.

Every thought produced by the conscious mind is clothed with an emotional statement, out of which likeness will be produced and will affect us. In his book Think and Grow Rich, the author says that there are Seven Major Positive Emotions. They are the emotions of desire, faith, love, sex, enthusiasm, romance, and hope. He also highlights Seven Major Negative Emotions: emotions of fear, jealousy, hatred, revenge, greed, superstition and anger. He says that these occupy the mind at all times, hence one or the other must dominate. These emotions are the fruits of the tree of good and evil. The tree is ever present and one must choose not to eat, for the temptation is always there: opportunities to strengthen ourselves.

An important duty of the conscious mind is to carefully examine and monitor the images it conceives, and to be aware of the emotion it attaches to these images before they enter the subconscious; for the subconscious does not discriminate, it willingly accepts without question and produces a true replica of what it receives.

Tilling the Soul

From time to time one wakes up from the sleep of habit to find and feel a sense of dissatisfaction in life, and the desire for change jars at the mind. Instituting change could be problematic, for habits or automatic operating systems stored in the subconscious resist change. Once these powerful systems of thought patterns and beliefs are entrenched, they become "You." Hence, to change, you are actually fighting against yourself, the one created by the conscious mind, the serpent of Genesis that you have allowed to become. In the beginning it was a potential, now it has become a principality in mind. The fight that takes place in mind between the man of the subconscious—the ego and the Christ man—is borne out in the wilderness narratives in the gospels. Jesus had just rediscovered his Christ self, and immediately after the battle for domination of his soul began, the contents of his subconscious mind began to surface and were in direct opposition to the desires of the Christ within him. This is the classic skirmish that goes on in every soul as it becomes aware that a change has to be made. It is a time when old beliefs must be discarded in order for newfound ones to take root. This process is what is termed forgiveness. It is the releasing of the emotions and labels previously cast into thought patterns and the spreading of the new, "One cannot put new wine in old wineskins," or "mend an old garment with new clothes." Jesus said to his disciples, "Go sell all that you have and then come and follow me." Forgiveness must become an ongoing practice in the constant renewing of the mind.

Jesus in the wilderness is an example of the process of this change process. Every time the devil (elements of the past) presented Jesus with emotionally filled thought patterns of the past, Jesus responded directly through the whisperings of the Christ: "Man shall not live by bread alone"; "You shall worship the Lord God and him only shall you serve"; "Thou shall not tempt the Lord your God."

The subconscious is never idle; it works twenty-four/seven, and one of its roles is to let us have all that we have asked for. It does not justify or question, it is solely in the production business. It transforms our wishes into tangible form so we might appreciate what we claim.

We might also liken the subconscious aspect of mind to the hard drive on a computer. In it is installed the operating system into which all other programs are placed and operate. We can install a system that says all things are possible and has the ability to accept new programs and also incorporates a built-in mode of obsolescence, or we can build one whose foundation is built on pure emotion that refuses to accept anything new.

When one relies on the subconscious to be the source of information, one will always be directed out of the past and will have repeated experiences. The conscious mind is pivotal, it has the ability to be directed by its Creator, by the subconscious, or it can rely on the serpent: the stimulants that come from the outer via the five senses. When fed directly and only by the Christ, the fruits produced will be perfect.

The law that governs the operations of the subconscious mind is belief. When we think or mentally form images in our minds from the pixels of energy that are always flowing in and through us, once we make the choice to accept these pictures, we name them by giving them an emotional code. This combination of thought and code finds its way, is stored, and over time will automatically produce a manifestation like unto itself. All beliefs are subjective, and limited, and not to be considered as truths.

We need to do forgiveness treatments in every conscious moment to clear away the powers and principalities of past, useless, harmful beliefs that reap havoc on our need to grow. We need to do as Abram did. After realizing that he had become a copy of his father, one who has become slothful, he got up with one thing in mind: to prosper, and immediately went out to find it. Because he allowed himself to be directed by his indwelling Christ, he encountered many conscious occurrences to reshape his thinking and over time became the dominating program that affected all his choices. Some beliefs he had to release were those of his father and two prominent relatives of his own, his wife, and contentiousness nephew, and covetousness.

If we are not willing to get out of the old country, we will repeat the same behavior over and over and our children will become carbon copies. A child's mind is sponge-like; it accepts and absorbs what is presented to him or her. Children see their caregivers as perfect role models and mold themselves after them, until they get older and see other forms they will not be able to seek different paths.

Life is a journey to the unknown, and all we have is the ability to create in the moment and expand as we do so. When we listen to the super-conscious, which is the way we are going, the only truth we should know and the only life or movement in which we should engage, then we will be operating out of the belief that, "The Lord shepherds me and I lack nothing." This is a powerful statement that must become the anchoring truth of one's life. The affirmation helps to set up an operating system in which the conscious mind is fed from spirit and what is being received goes directly to the subconscious; as a result all the fruits of the tree will be perfect, whole and complete. Then when the serpent, the stimuli that comes via the five senses as reflected through the subjective mind, will also be transformed, for the serpent feeds on the emotions of the subconscious.

Mistakes are oft repeated, for the sins/mistakes of the father/ original thought shall rest on the children/subconscious offspring even unto the tenth generation—for a very long time.

I draw this reference to acknowledge the words of Williams Wordsworth: "The child is father of the man." Our lives are reflections of the past information we store and hold to be true, and use to power our lives. We live out of the contents of the subconscious. Living out of the subconscious is like living out of a soup kitchen, having lost the power to feed yourself because you believe you cannot help yourself because you have told yourself that statement so often, you now believe it to be your truth. Soup kitchens are temporary; nothing is carved in stone unless it is decreed. The lies we put into the subconscious become the laws that govern our expressions and experiences. The contents of the subconscious become the traitors that betray us and cause us to suffer, and we move away from our Father's home.

Jesus was a great change agent, who realized that the people of his time wanted freedom from the Romans but were not willing to change their lives; hence he went face–to–face with the traditionalists who represent the old mindset, guided by old, outdated rites, rituals and convictions that might have worked centuries before in their tribal existence. His message was, change your mind; repent and experience the realm of perfection that is before you.

The programs of the subconscious are of a time past. They are no longer relevant, so one must remember to say to Satan—the false self that is individually built from old, worn-out thought patterns clothed with negative emotion—"Get thee behind me." Satan's intent might have been good if being stagnant is one's purpose, but the desire for an expanded consciousness outweighs the dissatisfaction one feels. "I will arise and go to my Father and I will say unto Him, Father I have made a mistake against heaven and before You; … Treat me as one of your hired servants." Both the conscious and subconscious are meant to serve the super-conscious, to express the divine potential that lies within.

Notes

_____

_____

_____

_____

_____

_____

_____

_____

_____

_____

Fifteen

The Power of Faith

By Rev. Alice J. Brown

In Matthew 9:27–31 (NRSV) Jesus heals two blind men, and in Verse 29 he said, "According to your faith be it done unto you" after touching their eyes. Then in Matthew 21:18–22 (NRSV), Jesus curses the fig tree and tells the disciples in Verse 21, "Truly

I tell you, if you have faith and do not doubt, not only will you do what has been done to the fig tree, but even if you say to this mountain, 'Be lifted up and thrown into the sea,' it will be done." And in Verse 22 he says, "Whatever you ask for in prayer with faith, you will receive." These are just a few of the scriptures that teach the power that lies within faith.

We will examine the power of faith in a variety of ways: scriptural and metaphysical definition, the difference between blind and understanding faith, the location of faith within each person, the size of it and how we can live our lives by faith rather than by sight, and truly know if it is faith or fear guiding our lives, thereby being able to make the appropriate adjustments where and when required.

Hebrew 11:1 (NRSV) gives a wonderful definition of faith, which is, "Now faith is the assurance of things hoped for, the conviction of things not seen." The entire eleventh chapter of Hebrews discusses the power of faith and how it was used by the Israelites such as Abraham and Moses, as well as other Israelite heroes. In the Revealing Word, Charles Fillmore gives the definition of faith as, "the perceiving power of the mind linked with the power to shape substance ... the power to do the seemingly impossible. It is a magnetic power that draws unto us our heart's desire from the invisible spiritual substance. Faith is a deep inner knowing that that which is sought is already ours for the taking." In Webster, faith is defined as, "belief and trust in and loyalty to God; belief in something for which there is no proof. Complete trust; something that is believed especially with strong conviction; especially a system of religious beliefs."

Begin to reflect upon these questions: What is faith to you? How do you use faith in your life? What do you believe in? Remember, according to your faith or belief system be it done unto you. This is powerful, because when Jesus performed a healing, this is what he told those he healed. Are you looking for a healing in your life, world and affairs? Do you believe you can be healed? Do you want to be healed?

Take a few moments to look at what you're having faith or belief in. Then think of the King James Version of Proverbs 23:7: "As he thinks in his heart so is he." It is significant to determine your belief system, because you cannot achieve your goals unless you are aware of your feelings, attitudes, opinions or memories. When you become aware of these things, you will know what has to be changed, if anything. Once you are knowledgeable of your belief system about any area of your life, you will know where the changes need to be made and how to go about making them. The good news is, there are tools you can work with to make adjustments where needed. Those tools are called denials, affirmations and forgiveness.

Denials and affirmations are known as the soap and water of the mind. When you deny that a situation or circumstance has any power over you, you are removing the negative belief about the facts from your subconscious mind. You are not denying that the facts exist; you are erasing or clearing old, worn-out beliefs about the facts. Once you make a denial, you must replace it with an affirmation or a positive prayer statement. You also forgive yourself and anyone else involved in the situation. These mental utensils can be used at any time. Once you begin to believe in yourself and your ability, you will be surprised how easy it will be to accomplish your goals. It will take time and work, but if you faint not and do not get weary, in due season your dreams will come true.

An ideal example of how you can accomplish your goals if you have faith and are willing to use it is the story of a young boy who grew up in a family where both of his parents were illiterate. They worked on a plantation in the Deep South, barely making a living. His father left the family in the South, and this young man, along with his siblings, had to work on the farm. He promised himself that when he grew up he would get a good education and treat his family better than he, his mother and siblings were treated. He held this picture in mind and believed he would accomplish his goal. He stayed in school, graduated from high school, went into the Marines during the Viet Nam war, married, had a family, and earned a college degree, all while working in factories and finally for a bus company, where he excelled. When he retired, he even had a nice sum of money saved. This young man kept his word; he treated his family much better than he had been treated. When asked how he was able to accomplish this goal, he said due to his faith in God and himself, he was able to keep the promise he had made so long ago to himself and to God. How powerful faith is when it is developed and used fully.

There are two types of faith: blind and understanding. Blind faith is faith based on spiritual principles; however, the main beliefs are not being used consciously. It still gets results, but the person using it does not necessarily know how to use it at will. "Understanding" faith, according to Charles Fillmore in The Revealing Word, is "Faith that functions from Principle. It is based on knowledge of Truth. It understands the law of mind action; therefore, it has great strength. To know that certain causes produce certain results gives a bedrock foundation for faith."

Journaling is a wonderful way to understand the difference between blind and understanding faith and to see just how faith works in your life. Take each situation you are dealing with, and pay close attention as to how you were able to handle the situation or to overcome in a particular area. Write down the steps employed and develop a road map of how you are recognizing and using the power of faith. As you continue to practice this technique, you will find you have a strategy for overcoming obstacles as they appear in your life. When a situation occurs, you will know what to do, for you can take your diary, follow the steps, and expand upon them.

Jesus is a good example to imitate when you are working to overcome a situation. First, he always prayed before attempting to do anything. Thus, let this be your model. Second,

201

he always gave thanks for answered prayer. Finally, he went about the task at hand with total confidence of the outcome. Always ask the question WWJD (What would Jesus do?). Don't just ask the question, answer the question by going to the gospels and reading how Jesus was able to accomplish the healings and miracles that he performed. Remember, he said we could do the things he did and even greater things.

Faith is also located within each of us at the pineal gland in the middle of the brain. It can be cultivated by concentrating our thoughts on this area and opening our minds to spiritual faith. This is done through prayer, meditation, and being in the silence. Dr. Donald Curtis gives the following meditation in Master Meditations as a means of developing spiritual faith: "I dwell in the consciousness of faith. The energy of the Spirit is permeating my thoughts, feelings and actions—all that I am. Thank You, God, for the privilege of faith. Thank You for the privilege of prayer. Thank You for the privilege of sharing. Thank You for the Light that moves through my being. Thank You for understanding." This is an affirmative statement that can be focused on daily. Not only that, but each of us can call faith forth at any time we desire it, especially since it is located within us and we do not have to look for it.

Yes, this powerful gift is available to us and we can use it at any time. We do not have to go outside ourselves to obtain it. Of course it is not as simple as it might sound, but it certainly can be done. It has to be practiced on a daily basis. Even when it might appear that your desire is not going to come into fruition, persevere. Stand firm and wait on the Lord. Yes, even if your body is racked with pain, know that health is your birthright and focus on your divinity. Mentally see yourself perfect, whole and complete. Spiritually speaking, you are. Don't give up until your body reflects the wholeness of your indwelling Christ. Speak the words of health, such as "I am health," as many times as necessary, until you begin to mentally see the perfection of God within you. Do all that you must do on the physical plane: go to the doctor, take your medication, and take proper care of yourself. You are a threefold being: spirit, soul, body. Have faith in the healing power of the Christ within you. Meditate on this scripture: "I lift up my eyes to the hills—from where will my help come? My help comes from the Lord, who made heaven and earth" (Psalms 121:1–2 NRSV).

Your health also comes from God, for you are made in His image and after His likeness. You are all that God is; recognize it, realize it, unify with it, and identify with it. Then, like Jesus, you too can say, "The Father and I are one" (John 10:30 NRSV). "The Father is in me and I am in the Father" (John 10:38 NRSV). Of course the ultimate is to have faith in God, not in the material or physical things that you can see. When you have faith in God, your total trust is in God. You know that God takes care of all that concerns you. As you develop the faith faculty that is within you, you turn everything over to God, knowing that it all works out for your highest good.

Reaching this level of spiritual growth is a process and takes time. Faith is a mighty gift, because just a little dab will do it, so to speak. Faith the size of a mustard seed will work wonders in your life, world and affairs. This is how the Reverend Dr. Johnnie Colemon described faith in the January 1996 edition of The Daily Inspiration: "Faith is sometimes called our spiritual eyes and spiritual fingers. This is the gift from God that enables us to see our good before it manifests, to call forth our dreams from the invisible, to shape and give form to the Substance of God that will become any manifest thing that we need or want. I like to talk about Substance as a big piece of dough that you can cut into any shape you want. The only limit is the limit you put on your own thinking."

When working with faith, it is imperative that we know the laws involved, which makes it easier to walk by faith rather than by sight. One law is the law of cause and effect, which simply says, "As within, so without." When one walks by faith they are like the woman with the issue of blood for twelve years, who knew all she had to do was touch Jesus' hem to be made whole. She pressed through the crowd and touched his hem; according to her belief she was healed. Think about this type of belief, and know that you too possess it.

What does walking by faith look like, you are asking, and how can it be accomplished on a daily basis? Walking by faith is not easy when those all around you are so heavily dealing with the facts and treating them as reality. Following is an excellent example of how you can walk by faith and not by sight even in the face of adversity.

The wallet of a young lady I know came up missing. The first thing she did after looking for it was prayed this prayer: "There is nothing lost in spirit." Then she mentally traced her steps to see if she could remember the last time she had the wallet. She made some calls to places she had visited, to see if the wallet had fallen out of her purse. She felt it had been lost, not stolen. She stood fast on this thought even when others attempted to tell her otherwise. This young lady continued to pray and mentally saw her wallet returned to her. Thirty days almost to the day that the wallet came up missing, it was returned to her. Someone found it and dropped it in a mailbox. She told me that the prayer has worked one hundred percent for her. She kept the faith even when others around her kept saying that it would not be returned. This person stated that she has used this prayer over twenty years and it had never failed her. Her faith was in the omnipresence of God and her oneness with the entire universe.

God knows everything, and is accessible to us all of the time. It is up to each person to constantly stay in contact with God, listen to what is being said, and to follow the guidance that is always given. On that note, this woman also confessed that if she had obeyed the inner instructions she had received, she would not have lost her wallet. A helpful formula when striving to follow God's guidance is to always "LOOK," which is an acronym for

"Listen, Observe, Obey, Know." Listen to what God is saying to you, observe what you hear, obey it once you understand what is being said, and know that you are following God's directions at all times. God is always talking to us in the "still, small voice." It is so quiet, it can be missed if we are not paying attention.

Walking by faith takes courage, especially when it seems you are the only one doing it. There are times when it is best not to share with others what you are doing until you receive the demonstration. The young woman with the missing wallet only told those who needed to know, so she would not have to listen to a lot of people attempting to convince her the wallet was lost forever. Of course, wisdom was used and steps were taken to report missing cards, replace licenses, and so forth. But the person kept affirming the truth: "Faith knows that a thing is so, before it appears on the physical plane."

As you are striving to work with faith, ask yourself this question, "Am I working with faith or fear?" Remember that you want to have faith in God, yet your faith works according to your belief. Do you believe or do you fear? Do you trust God or are you afraid to go for your dream? Think about Peter, who got out of the boat and walked on water toward Jesus. This took faith and courage. As long as he kept his attention on Jesus, he was certainly walking by faith and not by sight. Once he looked down he began to sink, and had to ask Jesus to save him (Matthew 14:28–30).

Are you willing to take a chance on doing something you want to do, but are afraid to do? Remember, faith is called, "spiritual eyes and spiritual fingers." Therefore, use your power of imagination to hold the picture of your desire in your mind and mentally see it coming into visibility.

How strong is your belief in yourself and your ability to achieve? If you have doubt, fear and low self-esteem, you will not be able to accomplish your desires unless you are willing to make the appropriate changes. It will take time and work, however. The Reverend Dr. Johnnie Colemon would always tell her congregation, "It works if you work it." Are you willing to move from fear to faith?

You can flip the script. You don't have to remain where you are; you can become a new creation in Christ Jesus. Push through the crowd of negativity. Sit quietly and see yourself accomplishing your goals. What is it that you want to do? See yourself doing it, and then begin to take steps to accomplish your dream. There was a janitor who worked in a doctor's office. He had a goal of becoming a doctor. While he worked, he saw himself doing that which he desired. He went to the library and studied. He enrolled in night school and continued to work, until one day his dream became a reality. He was willing to do what it took to become the person he dreamed he would be. God is no respecter of persons. What is done for one can and will be done for all. Just begin to move forward toward your goal.

A minister once shared that she had been called to the ministry when she was young. She knew as a child that she had a gift of healing. She intuitively knew this, even though she did not fully understand what it meant. She kept it a secret for a long time, but she always had a wonderful relationship with God. She grew up prior to women's rights, and was not encouraged to become a minister. She also knew she wanted to get her education, get married, have children, and accomplish other goals, which she did. However, her faith in her calling was strong, and eventually she began to develop this calling. She finally reached her goal, was ordained in 1995, and has been ministering ever since.

To tell the truth, she said she was ministering all of her life, just not officially as the world would recognize, but wanted to pastor a church. For a great while, she allowed doubt, fear and low self-esteem to stop her in that goal, the feeling that she was not smart enough, or good enough. Then one day she walked into Christ Universal Temple, where the minister was the Reverend Dr. Johnnie Colemon. Dr. Colemon taught her she could overcome any obstacles and obtain her dream. While there, the woman met the Reverend Dr. Helen Carry, who was second-in-command to Dr. Colemon, and found a role model. Dr. Carry was a wife and mother like her, and had a successful career. In Dr. Carry, the woman saw a person who had followed God's calling and was now teaching others that they, too, could accomplish their dreams. Her faith renewed, she began to dream of possibilities for herself.

She stepped out on faith and went for the goal, and she has not looked back since.

Of course it was not easy and she had to work quite hard. Yet, today she is the pastor of a church and is making great strides. She says there are still times when doubts, fears and even low self-esteem come, but she works within her mind, praying, meditating and listening to God. She is willing to follow what God tells her to do, most of the time. This minister stated that she is still not where she wants to be, but praise God she is far from where she started. Yes, there are times when she has to flip the script, for she was the first in her family of origin to earn a college degree and have a career. There are times when she feels she should not be where she is. However, this woman is on a mission and has committed her life to teaching others how they too can use the power of faith to live healthy, happy and prosperous lives.

Faith is the power to do the seemingly impossible, but with God all things are possible. All of us are powerhouses; like this minister, we all have spiritual gifts within us waiting for us to develop and bring forward. Yes, it takes time, energy, and most of all faith to do what God has ordained us to do. It is up to each person to recognize that faith is a faculty within them, but it only takes a small amount to do a great job if we can walk by faith instead of by sight, and if we do not let fear overtake us and cause us to be wimps instead of heroes.

The world is calling for God's people to let it be known that God created us just a little lower than the angels, and it is up to us to allow the Spirit of God to express through us out into the world. Faith is the power to make it so. Dare to live your dreams. Dare to let your light shine for the world to see.

Resources

Curtis, Donald. Master Meditations. Santa Monica: IBS, Inc. 1990

Cady, H. Emilie. Lessons in Truth. Unity Village: Unity Books, 1903; 1995

Fillmore, Charles. The Revealing Word. Unity Village: Unity Books, 1959; 1994

Brown, Alice J. January Daily Inspiration. Chicago: Universal Foundation for Better Living, Inc., 1996

Brown, Alice J. March Daily Inspiration. Chicago: Universal Foundation for Better Living, Inc., 2010

The Holy Bible, NRSV, King James Version

Notes

Sixteen

The Financial Principles of Sowing & Reaping

By Robert Henderson Jr. CFP ®

The financial principles of sowing and reaping are founded on the basis that you must first sow before you can reap. To sow means to plant, and whatever we plant (think or do), it will return to us, this law works regardless of what you plant, good or bad. This is the law of mutual exchange. Any person who contributes to prosperity must prosper him or herself. No man can get rich unless he enriches others. To reap means to receive. You can only receive that which you put out (plant), be it good or bad; nothing's free. You shall only receive what you put out, for this is the law. The laws of nature have been written by the Creator of the universe. Everything you do and everything you believe has repercussions. In other words, be careful of what you think and especially careful about what you believe. Your beliefs navigate your life actions. What is done throughout a person's life will

absolutely affect his or her life, both here on earth and forever after.

Many people continue to struggle through life, never realizing or understanding the principle laws of the universe. The law of mutual exchange (sowing and reaping) should be taught as required learning in early grade school. It should rank next to a child learning how to read.

Sowing and reaping is the law of the harvest. Harvest means to receive, to gather, to gain, to win, to acquire. In other words, harvest means to reap. The law of the harvest is a principle, and the principle says: plant little, harvests little; plant much, harvest much. Again, it's a law of mutual exchange, a powerful and perfect law that never fails. In fact, it's so exact, it will work with any resource, whether it's your time, your talents, your tithes, and especially your love. You will always get what you have sown. If you want love, you can't plant hate. If you want prosperity, you can't plant fear-and-poverty thoughts in your subconscious mind.

Again, for whatever you plant, you shall receive like kind in your world and affairs. Trust me, nothing comes into existence in and of itself—every effect has a corresponding cause. This law is true in the physical world as well as the spiritual. We cannot get something or receive something for nothing. Any attempt at getting something for nothing is a violation of the law, and not just man's law, but universal law. Many people find themselves in prison and down and out for thinking they could break the law, but in truth, they only break themselves.

We cannot receive anything without paying a price. To become a top-notch medical doctor, you must invest long years of difficult study. To become a top actor, you must invest lots of time and long hours reading, studying and performing well in order to reach star status with top pay. Whether your goal is to become a movie star or minister, an educator or athlete, you will reap what you have sown. In other words, you must pay a price before you see a harvest. For this is the law. If you take the time and study these laws, understand how they work and let them work for you, your entire life and affairs will change to your heart's desires. This is not only a promise, this is the law.

Another thing, just in case some of you might be from the world of instant gratification: sowing and reaping usually don't happen on the same day, any more than when a farmer plants corn. It would be ludicrous for the farmer to expect a harvest later that day, because he knows there is a season for everything. Yet if you take the time and study these laws, understand how they work and let them work for you, your entire life and affairs will change to your heart's desires. This is not only a promise, this is the law.

Plant on, my brothers and sisters.

Notes

- Seventeen -
Self Discipline
Is the Key

By Robert Henderson Jr. CFP®

Self-discipline is the key to change. If you want more, if you want better, if you want to learn, study, and grow, mastering your impulses and controlling your emotions must be on lockdown. Self-discipline is a prerequisite for achieving success in virtually every aspect of life. Whether you are pursuing career goals or changing personal habits, you must learn self-discipline. Think of self-discipline as having the ability to make yourself do all the things you know you ought to do, when you don't feel like doing them. Wow! Don't read past that last sentence too fast, stop and take a moment to study what I've just said. Look at your life as you currently see it; imagine how much more rewarding and fulfilling it could be if only you would do all the things you know you ought to do. Understanding the power of self-discipline should be a required study in early childhood learning, and should be taught, studied and examined in every classroom before a child

is allowed to graduate from high school. Sadly, not everyone who turns twenty-one and enters into adulthood enters with this skill in place.

The good news is, it's a skill that's never too late to begin to learn.

Self-discipline is indeed a learned skill. Some of us learn it naturally at an early age, but it's obvious that millions of us don't, and as a result often face difficulties and challenges in life. (Prisons and jails are full with those who lack self-discipline).

Many people are forever learning and studying, but never come to the realization of truth. In a similar way, we often try to control others, but according to universal law, before man can truly gain the power to master forces and things, he must gain the power to master and control himself.

Many people say they know the truth, but are unable to demonstrate the truth. We know this because many people say one thing, yet do another. We are what we think and do all day long. In order to begin training yourself—and oh yes, it is training—you must begin by first accomplishing small goals. Then, gradually increase the level of difficulty as your self-discipline improves.

If this sounds too simple, be aware that self-discipline is the key strategy used by all superstars—those who have achieved great success, perhaps even fame, in their chosen professions. A superstar might have a trainer or a manager or coach who consistently gets on his back and makes him do the things he needs to do. Actually, no one can truly make another do what they don't want to do: maybe physically, but definitely not mentally. And self-discipline is totally mental. Though it might be a boost to have another person remind and goad us when we begin to falter, a person wanting to gain self-discipline needs only their mind, and faith they can accomplish the goal.

Warning: Self-discipline isn't something you achieve overnight. It must be learned, you have to want it, and want it real bad.

The first step you must take toward acquiring self-discipline is to ask for it. As the scripture says, ask, and it shall be given you; Pray, meditate and concentrate, and think on that which you want to achieve. Imagine yourself being disciplined about whatever it is you want to accomplish. You have to train yourself to see yourself exactly as you want to be. Your mind must move from the thought to the thing. Act as though "I am," and "I will be." You have to really believe it is done before the law of belief will release it from the inner world (invisible world) into the outer world (visible world).

Oh yeah, there is a law of belief, just like there's the law of gravity. The great Creator of the heaven, the earth and the universe set up all these laws that govern all of creation. Sadly, many people either don't know or even believe these laws exist. No wonder so many have come to believe that their lives are shaped by outer conditions and circumstances. You must truly believe, not with mere words, but your belief must be felt and impressed on your subconscious mind.

The next step after asking is to seek. To seek is to be in search of: to seek the kingdom, to seek the truth. According to the law, it is impossible to truly seek and not find. The scriptures say *seek, and ye shall find.* Not, *seek and you might find,* but *seek—ye shall find.* The problem is, most people are seeking the wrong things. Most people seek material things, things that perish and fade away. If you ask and then seek self-discipline, you would have the mind to obtain anything your heart desires, including material things.

The next and final step to obtaining self-discipline is to knock. Knock and it shall be open to you, the Bible says. Some of you might ask, "What shall be open to you?" The answer is, what do you want? Where are you going? In other words, what are your goals? Self-discipline is only needed by those of us who have an aim to achieve something—to become successful at something. We define success as the progressive realization of a worthy goal. Anyone who has set a worthy goal for himself, and is progressively working toward achieving it, is a success. And in order to become successful of achieving a worthy goal, you must have self-discipline, for this is the law. The good news is, anyone who has a desire and the will to discipline him or herself is knocking on the doors of unlimited possibilities. Prepare to soar.

Notes

_____

_____

_____

_____

_____

_____

_____

_____

_____

_____

Author Contact Information

Rev. Dr. Mary A. Tumpkin
Universal Truth Center for
Better Living
21310 N.W. 37th Avenue
Miami Gardens, Florida 33056
305.624.4991
www.utruthcenter.org
mtumpkin@aol.com

Rev. Dr. Emma Luster-Lassiter
www.lovewisdomell.cs.com
Elder Reginald Torian
Christ Universal Temple
11901 S. Ashland Avenue
Chicago, IL 606
reginaldtorian@yahoo.com
lovewisdomell@cs.com

Rev. Evan Reid
Verity Centre For Better Living
28 Milford Avenue
Toronto, ON M6M 2V8 Canada
416.240.1956
www.veritycentre.org
admin@veritycentre.org

Rev. Alice J. Brown
Living Truth Center for
Better Living, Inc.
1850 Belmore Road
East Cleveland, Ohio 44112
216.249.0330
www.livingtruthcenter.org
uoom@aol.com

Robert Henderson Jr. CFP ®
The Henderson Financial Group
5783A NW 151st Street
Miami Lakes, FL 33014
(305) 825-1444
www.roberthendersonjr.com
www.newundergroundrailroad.com

Rev. Dr. Anna M. Price
Universal Truth Center for
Better Living
21310 N.W. 37th Avenue
Miami Gardens, Florida 33056
305.624.4991
www.utruthcenter.org
aprice55@aol.com

Rev. Derrick B. Wells
Christ Universal Temple
11901 S. Ashland Avenue
Chicago, IL 60643
773.568.2282
www.cutemple.org
revwells@cutemple.org

The Healing Ministries of the
Rev. Eric Ovid Donaldson
Senior Minister
Unity Christian Church
3345 McCorkle Road
Memphis, TN 38116
901-461-3403
www.unitychristianchurch.us
www.thehealingministries.net
www.facebook.com/rev.donaldson
www.facebook.com/UnityChristianChurch
newthoughthealer@gmail.com

Rev. Bernette L. Jones
One God One Thought Center
for Better Living
3605 Coronado Road.
Baltimore, Maryland 21244
410.496.5188
www.ogot.org
bjones927@aol.com

Notes

_____

_____

_____

_____

_____

_____

_____

_____

_____

_____

Notes

Notes

_____

_____

_____

_____

_____

_____

_____

_____

_____

_____

_____

Notes

Made in the USA
Charleston, SC
28 September 2012